PRAXIS

ENGLISH TO SPEAKERS OF OTHER LANGUAGES (ESOL) 0361

By: Sharon Wynne, M.S.

XAMonline, INC.
Boston

To obtain permission(s) to use the material from this work for any purpose including workshops or seminars, please submit a written request to:

XAMonline, Inc.
25 First Street, Suite 106
Cambridge, MA 02141
Toll Free 1-800-301-4647
Email: info@xamonline.com
Web: www.xamonline.com
Fax: 1-617-583-5552

Library of Congress Cataloging-in-Publication Data

Wynne, Sharon A.
    PRAXIS English to Speakers of Other Languages (ESOL) 0361 /
    Sharon A. Wynne. 3rd ed.
    ISBN 978-1-60787-348-8
    1. English to Speakers of Other Languages (ESOL) 0361
    2. Study Guides
    3. PRAXIS
    4. Teachers' Certification & Licensure
    5. Careers

Disclaimer:

The opinions expressed in this publication are the sole works of XAMonline and were created independently from the National Education Association, Educational Testing Service, or any State Department of Education, National Evaluation Systems or other testing affiliates.

Between the time of publication and printing, state specific standards as well as testing formats and Web site information may change and therefore would not be included in part or in whole within this product. Sample test questions are developed by XAMonline and reflect content similar to that on real tests; however, they are not former test questions. XAMonline assembles content that aligns with state standards but makes no claims nor guarantees teacher candidates a passing score. Numerical scores are determined by testing companies such as NES or ETS and then are compared with individual state standards. A passing score varies from state to state.

Printed in the United States of America   œ-1

PRAXIS English to Speakers of Other Languages (ESOL) 0361
ISBN: 978-1-60787-348-8

Table of Contents

COMPETENCY 8
MATERIALS

COMPETENCY 9
MANAGING THE CLASSROOM AND STUDENTS

DOMAIN IV
ASSESSMENT

COMPETENCY 10
KNOWLEDGE OF TESTS AND STANDARDS

COMPETENCY 14

COMPETENCY 15

COMPETENCY 16

SAMPLE TEST

PRAXIS

PRAXIS ENGLISH TO SPEAKERS OF OTHER LANGUAGES (ESOL) 0361

SECTION 1
ABOUT XAMONLINE

XAMonline—A Specialty Teacher Certification Company

Created in 1996, XAMonline was the first company to publish study guides for state-specific teacher certification examinations. Founder Sharon Wynne found it frustrating that materials were not available for teacher certification preparation and decided to create the first single, state-specific guide. XAMonline has grown into a company of over 1,800 contributors and writers and offers over 300 titles for the entire PRAXIS series and every state examination. No matter what state you plan on teaching in, XAMonline has a unique teacher certification study guide just for you.

XAMonline—Value and Innovation

We are committed to providing value and innovation. Our print-on-demand technology allows us to be the first in the market to reflect changes in test standards and user feedback as they occur. Our guides are written by experienced teachers who are experts in their fields. And our content reflects the highest standards of quality. Comprehensive practice tests with varied levels of rigor means that your study experience will closely match the actual in-test experience.

To date, XAMonline has helped nearly 600,000 teachers pass their certification or licensing exams. Our commitment to preparation exceeds simply providing the proper material for study—it extends to helping teachers **gain mastery** of the subject matter, giving them the **tools** to become the most effective classroom leaders possible, and ushering today's students toward a **successful future**.

SECTION 2
ABOUT THIS STUDY GUIDE

Purpose of This Guide

Is there a little voice inside of you saying, "Am I ready?" Our goal is to replace that little voice and remove all doubt with a new voice that says, "I AM READY. **Bring it on!**" by offering the highest quality of teacher certification study guides.

Organization of Content

You will see that while every test may start with overlapping general topics, each is very unique in the skills they wish to test. Only XAMonline presents custom content that analyzes deeper than a title, a subarea, or an objective. Only XAMonline presents content and sample test assessments along with **focus statements**, the deepest-level rationale and interpretation of the skills that are unique to the exam.

Title and field number of test

→Each exam has its own name and number. XAMonline's guides are written to give you the content you need to know for the specific exam you are taking. You can be confident when you buy our guide that it contains the information you need to study for the specific test you are taking.

Subareas

→These are the major content categories found on the exam. XAMonline's guides are written to cover all of the subareas found in the test frameworks developed for the exam.

Objectives

→These are standards that are unique to the exam and represent the main subcategories of the subareas/content categories. XAMonline's guides are written to address every specific objective required to pass the exam.

Focus statements

→These are examples and interpretations of the objectives. You find them in parenthesis directly following the objective. They provide detailed examples of the range, type, and level of content that appear on the test questions. **Only XAMonline's guides drill down to this level.**

How Do We Compare with Our Competitors?

XAMonline—drills down to the focus statement level.
CliffsNotes and REA—organized at the objective level
Kaplan—provides only links to content
MoMedia—content not specific to the state test

Each subarea is divided into manageable sections that cover the specific skill areas. Explanations are easy to understand and thorough. You'll find that every test answer contains a rejoinder so if you need a refresher or further review after taking the test, you'll know exactly to which section you must return.

How to Use This Book

Our informal polls show that most people begin studying up to eight weeks prior to the test date, so start early. Then ask yourself some questions: How much do you really know? Are you coming to the test straight from your teacher-education program or are you having to review subjects you haven't considered in ten years? Either way, take a **diagnostic or assessment test** first. Also, spend time on sample tests so that you become accustomed to the way the actual test will appear.

This guide comes with an online diagnostic test of 30 questions found online at *www.XAMonline.com*. It is a little boot camp to get you up for the task and reveal things about your compendium of knowledge in general. Although this guide is structured to follow the order of the test, you are not required to study in that order. By finding a time-management and study plan that fits your life you will be more effective. The results of your diagnostic or self-assessment test can be a guide for how to manage your time and point you toward an area that needs more attention.

After taking the diagnostic exam, fill out the **Personalized Study Plan** page at the beginning of each chapter. Review the competencies and skills covered in that chapter and check the boxes that apply to your study needs. If there are sections you already know you can skip, check the "skip it" box. Taking this step will give you a study plan for each chapter.

Week	Activity
8 weeks prior to test	Take a diagnostic test found at www.XAMonline.com
7 weeks prior to test	Build your Personalized Study Plan for each chapter. Check the "skip it" box for sections you feel you are already strong in. ✗ SKIP IT ☐
6-3 weeks prior to test	For each of these four weeks, choose a content area to study. You don't have to go in the order of the book. It may be that you start with the content that needs the most review. Alternately, you may want to ease yourself into plan by starting with the most familiar material.
2 weeks prior to test	Take the sample test, score it, and create a review plan for the final week before the test.
1 week prior to test	Following your plan (which will likely be aligned with the areas that need the most review) go back and study the sections that align with the questions you may have gotten wrong. Then go back and study the sections related to the questions you answered correctly. If need be, create flashcards and drill yourself on any area that you makes you anxious.

SECTION 3
ABOUT THE PRAXIS EXAMS

What Is PRAXIS?

PRAXIS II tests measure the knowledge of specific content areas in K-12 education. The test is a way of insuring that educators are prepared to not only teach in a particular subject area, but also have the necessary teaching skills to be effective. The Educational Testing Service administers the test in most states and has worked with the states to develop the material so that it is appropriate for state standards.

PRAXIS Points

1. The PRAXIS Series comprises more than 140 different tests in over 70 different subject areas.

2. Over 90% of the PRAXIS tests measure subject area knowledge.

3. The purpose of the test is to measure whether the teacher candidate possesses a sufficient level of knowledge and skills to perform job duties effectively and responsibly.

4. Your state sets the acceptable passing score.

5. Any candidate, whether from a traditional teaching-preparation path or an alternative route, can seek to enter the teaching profession by taking a PRAXIS test.

6. PRAXIS tests are updated regularly to ensure current content.

Often **your own state's requirements** determine whether or not you should take any particular test. The most reliable source of information regarding this is your state's Department of Education. This resource should have a complete list of testing centers and dates. Test dates vary by subject area and not all test dates necessarily include your particular test, so be sure to check carefully.

If you are in a teacher-education program, check with the Education Department or the Certification Officer for specific information for testing and testing timelines. The Certification Office should have most of the information you need.

If you choose an alternative route to certification you can either rely on our website at *www.XAMonline.com* or on the resources provided by an alternative certification program. Many states now have specific agencies devoted to alternative certification and there are some national organizations as well, for example:

National Association for Alternative Certification
http://www.alt-teachercert.org/index.asp

Interpreting Test Results

Contrary to what you may have heard, the results of a PRAXIS test are not based on time. More accurately, you will be scored on the raw number of points you earn in relation to the raw number of points available. Each question is worth one raw point. It is likely to your benefit to complete as many questions in the time allotted, but it will not necessarily work to your advantage if you hurry through the test.

Follow the guidelines provided by ETS for interpreting your score. The web site offers a sample test score sheet and clearly explains how the scores are scaled and what to expect if you have an essay portion on your test.

Scores are usually available by phone within a month of the test date and scores will be sent to your chosen institution(s) within six weeks. Additionally, ETS now makes online, downloadable reports available for 45 days from the reporting date.

It is **critical** that you be aware of your own state's passing score. Your raw score may qualify you to teach in some states, but not all. ETS administers the test and assigns a score, but the states make their own interpretations and, in some cases, consider combined scores if you are testing in more than one area.

What's on the Test?

The Praxis English to Speakers of Other Languages (ESOL) 0361 exam lasts 2 hours and consists of two sections, each with multiple-choice questions. The breakdown of the questions is as follows:

Category	Approximate Number of Questions	Approximate Percentage of the Test
Section One: Listening Section	20	17%
I: Oral Grammar and Vocabulary		
II: Pronunciation		

Continued on next page

Section Two: Standard Section		
I: Foundations of Linguistics and Language Learning	28	23%
II: Planning, Implementing, and Managing Instruction	36	30%
III: Assessment	18	15%
IV: Cultural and Professional Aspects of the Job	18	15%

Question Types

You're probably thinking, enough already, I want to study! Indulge us a little longer while we explain that there is actually more than one type of multiple-choice question. You can thank us later after you realize how well prepared you are for your exam.

1. Complete the Statement. The name says it all. In this question type you'll be asked to choose the correct completion of a given statement. For example:

> **The Dolch Basic Sight Words consist of a relatively short list of words that children should be able to:**
>
>   A. Sound out
>
>   B. Know the meaning of
>
>   C. Recognize on sight
>
>   D. Use in a sentence

The correct answer is C. In order to check your answer, test out the statement by adding the choices to the end of it.

2. Which of the Following. One way to test your answer choice for this type of question is to replace the phrase "which of the following" with your selection. Use this example:

> **Which of the following words is one of the twelve most frequently used in children's reading texts:**
>
>   A. There
>
>   B. This
>
>   C. The
>
>   D. An

Don't look! Test your answer. _____ is one of the twelve most frequently used in children's reading texts. Did you guess C? Then you guessed correctly.

3. Roman Numeral Choices. This question type is used when there is more than one possible correct answer. For example:

> **Which of the following two arguments accurately supports the use of cooperative learning as an effective method of instruction?**
>
> I. Cooperative learning groups facilitate healthy competition between individuals in the group.
> II. Cooperative learning groups allow academic achievers to carry or cover for academic underachievers.
> III. Cooperative learning groups make each student in the group accountable for the success of the group.
> IV. Cooperative learning groups make it possible for students to reward other group members for achieving.
>
> A. I and II
> B. II and III
> C. I and III
> D. III and IV

Notice that the question states there are **two** possible answers. It's best to read all the possibilities first before looking at the answer choices. In this case, the correct answer is D.

4. Negative Questions. This type of question contains words such as "not," "least," and "except." Each correct answer will be the statement that does **not** fit the situation described in the question. Such as:

> **Multicultural education is not**
>
> A. An idea or concept
> B. A "tack-on" to the school curriculum
> C. An educational reform movement
> D. A process

Think to yourself that the statement could be anything but the correct answer. This question form is more open to interpretation than other types, so read carefully and don't forget that you're answering a negative statement.

5. **Questions that Include Graphs, Tables, or Reading Passages.** As always, read the question carefully. It likely asks for a very specific answer and not a broad interpretation of the visual. Here is a simple (though not statistically accurate) example of a graph question:

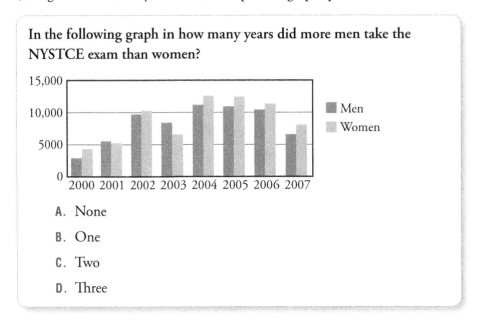

In the following graph in how many years did more men take the NYSTCE exam than women?

A. None

B. One

C. Two

D. Three

It may help you to simply circle the two years that answer the question. Make sure you've read the question thoroughly and once you've made your determination, double check your work. The correct answer is C.

SECTION 4
HELPFUL HINTS

Study Tips

1. **You are what you eat.** Certain foods aid the learning process by releasing natural memory enhancers called CCKs (cholecystokinin) composed of tryptophan, choline, and phenylalanine. All of these chemicals enhance the neurotransmitters associated with memory and certain foods release memory

enhancing chemicals. A light meal or snacks of one of the following foods fall into this category:

- Milk
- Rice
- Eggs
- Fish
- Nuts and seeds
- Oats
- Turkey

The better the connections, the more you comprehend!

2. **See the forest for the trees.** In other words, get the concept before you look at the details. One way to do this is to take notes as you read, paraphrasing or summarizing in your own words. Putting the concept in terms that are comfortable and familiar may increase retention.

3. **Question authority.** Ask why, why, why? Pull apart written material paragraph by paragraph and don't forget the captions under the illustrations. For example, if a heading reads *Stream Erosion* put it in the form of a question (Why do streams erode? What is stream erosion?) then find the answer within the material. If you train your mind to think in this manner you will learn more and prepare yourself for answering test questions.

4. **Play mind games.** Using your brain for reading or puzzles keeps it flexible. Even with a limited amount of time your brain can take in data (much like a computer) and store it for later use. In ten minutes you can: read two paragraphs (at least), quiz yourself with flash cards, or review notes. Even if you don't fully understand something on the first pass, your mind stores it for recall, which is why frequent reading or review increases chances of retention and comprehension.

5. **Get pointed in the right direction.** Use arrows to point to important passages or pieces of information. It's easier to read than a page full of yellow highlights. Highlighting can be used sparingly, but add an arrow to the margin to call attention to it.

6. **Place yourself in exile and set the mood.** Set aside a particular place and time to study that best suits your personal needs and biorhythms. If you're a night person, burn the midnight oil. If you're a morning person set yourself up with some coffee and get to it. Make your study time and place as free from distraction as possible and surround yourself with what you need, be it silence or music. Studies have shown that music can aid in concentration, absorption, and retrieval of information. Not all music, though. Classical music is said to work best

7. **The pen is mightier than the sword.** Learn to take great notes. A by-product of our modern culture is that we have grown accustomed to getting our information in short doses. We've subconsciously trained ourselves to assimilate information into neat little packages. Messy notes fragment the flow of information. Your notes can be much clearer with proper formatting. *The Cornell Method* is one such format. This method was popularized in *How to Study in College*, Ninth Edition, by Walter Pauk. You can benefit from the method without purchasing an additional book by simply looking up the method online. Below is a sample of how *The Cornell Method* can be adapted for use with this guide.

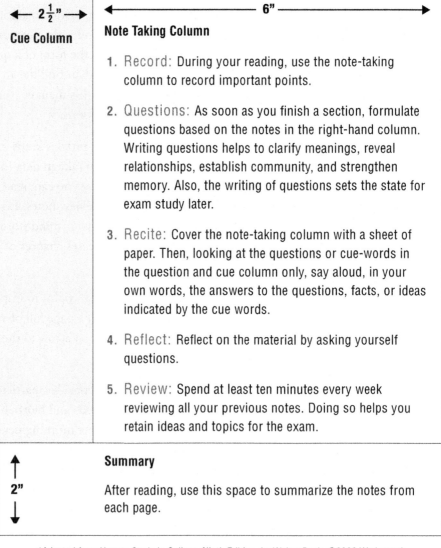

← 2½″ → **Cue Column**	←——————— 6″ ———————→ **Note Taking Column** 1. Record: During your reading, use the note-taking column to record important points. 2. Questions: As soon as you finish a section, formulate questions based on the notes in the right-hand column. Writing questions helps to clarify meanings, reveal relationships, establish community, and strengthen memory. Also, the writing of questions sets the state for exam study later. 3. Recite: Cover the note-taking column with a sheet of paper. Then, looking at the questions or cue-words in the question and cue column only, say aloud, in your own words, the answers to the questions, facts, or ideas indicated by the cue words. 4. Reflect: Reflect on the material by asking yourself questions. 5. Review: Spend at least ten minutes every week reviewing all your previous notes. Doing so helps you retain ideas and topics for the exam.
↑ 2″ ↓	**Summary** After reading, use this space to summarize the notes from each page.

*Adapted from How to Study in College, Ninth Edition, by Walter Pauk, ©2008 Wadsworth

8. Check your budget. You should at least review all the content material before your test, but allocate the most amount of time to the areas that need the most refreshing. It sounds obvious, but it's easy to forget. You can use the study rubric above to balance your study budget.

The proctor will write the start time where it can be seen and then, later, provide the time remaining, typically fifteen minutes before the end of the test.

Testing Tips

1. Get smart, play dumb. Sometimes a question is just a question. No one is out to trick you, so don't assume that the test writer is looking for something other than what was asked. Stick to the question as written and don't overanalyze.

2. Do a double take. Read test questions and answer choices at least twice because it's easy to miss something, to transpose a word or some letters. If you have no idea what the correct answer is, skip it and come back later if there's time. If you're still clueless, it's okay to guess. Remember, you're scored on the number of questions you answer correctly and you're not penalized for wrong answers. The worst case scenario is that you miss a point from a good guess.

3. Turn it on its ear. The syntax of a question can often provide a clue, so make things interesting and turn the question into a statement to see if it changes the meaning or relates better (or worse) to the answer choices.

4. Get out your magnifying glass. Look for hidden clues in the questions because it's difficult to write a multiple-choice question without giving away part of the answer in the options presented. In most questions you can readily eliminate one or two potential answers, increasing your chances of answering correctly to 50/50, which will help out if you've skipped a question and gone back to it (see tip #2).

5. Call it intuition. Often your first instinct is correct. If you've been studying the content you've likely absorbed something and have subconsciously retained the knowledge. On questions you're not sure about trust your instincts because a first impression is usually correct.

6. Graffiti. Sometimes it's a good idea to mark your answers directly on the test booklet and go back to fill in the optical scan sheet later. You don't get extra points for perfectly blackened ovals. If you choose to manage your test this way, be sure not to mismark your answers when you transcribe to the scan sheet.

7. **Become a clock-watcher.** You have a set amount of time to answer the questions. Don't get bogged down laboring over a question you're not sure about when there are ten others you could answer more readily. If you choose to follow the advice of tip #6, be sure you leave time near the end to go back and fill in the scan sheet.

Do the Drill

No matter how prepared you feel it's sometimes a good idea to apply Murphy's Law. So the following tips might seem silly, mundane, or obvious, but we're including them anyway.

1. **Remember, you are what you eat, so bring a snack.** Choose from the list of energizing foods that appear earlier in the introduction.

2. **You're not too sexy for your test.** Wear comfortable clothes. You'll be distracted if your belt is too tight or if you're too cold or too hot.

3. **Lie to yourself.** Even if you think you're a prompt person, pretend you're not and leave plenty of time to get to the testing center. Map it out ahead of time and do a dry run if you have to. There's no need to add road rage to your list of anxieties.

4. **Bring sharp number 2 pencils.** It may seem impossible to forget this need from your school days, but you might. And make sure the erasers are intact, too.

5. **No ticket, no test.** Bring your admission ticket as well as **two** forms of identification, including one with a picture and signature. You will not be admitted to the test without these things.

6. **You can't take it with you.** Leave any study aids, dictionaries, notebooks, computers, and the like at home. Certain tests **do** allow a scientific or four-function calculator, so check ahead of time to see if your test does.

7. **Prepare for the desert.** Any time spent on a bathroom break **cannot** be made up later, so use your judgment on the amount you eat or drink.

8. **Quiet, Please!** Keeping your own time is a good idea, but not with a timepiece that has a loud ticker. If you use a watch, take it off and place it nearby but not so that it distracts you. And **silence your cell phone**.

To the best of our ability, we have compiled the content you need to know in this book and in the accompanying online resources. The rest is up to you. You can use the study and testing tips or you can follow your own methods. Either way, you can be confident that there aren't any missing pieces of information and there shouldn't be any surprises in the content on the test.

If you have questions about test fees, registration, electronic testing, or other content verification issues please visit *www.ets.org*.

Good luck!

Sharon Wynne
Founder, XAMonline

PRAXIS

DOMAIN I
LISTENING SECTION

PERSONALIZED STUDY PLAN

KNOWN MATERIAL/ SKIP IT

PAGE	COMPETENCY	
3	1A: Oral Grammar and Vocabulary	☐
3	1B: Pronunciation	☐

COMPETENCY 1

PART A ORAL GRAMMAR AND VOCABULARY

Visit *www.xamonline.com* for an audio file that will aid you in practicing for the listening portion of the Praxis ESOL 0361 exam.

PART B PRONUNCIATION

Visit *www.xamonline.com* for an audio file that will aid you in practicing for the listening portion of the Praxis ESOL 0361 exam.

DOMAIN II
FOUNDATIONS OF LINGUISTICS AND LANGUAGE LEARNING

PERSONALIZED STUDY PLAN

KNOWN MATERIAL/ SKIP IT

COMPETENCY 2
LINGUISTIC THEORY

SKILL 2.1 **Phonetic transcription and terminology, stress and intonation patterns, and the effects of phonetic environment on pronunciation**

The definition of **PHONOLOGY** can be summarized as "the way in which speech sounds form patterns" (Díaz-Rico and Weed, 1995). Phonology is a subset of the linguistics field, which studies the organization and systems of sound within a particular language. Phonology is based on the theory that every native speaker unconsciously retains the sound structure of that language and is more concerned with the sounds than with the physical process of creating those sounds.

When babies babble or make what we call "baby talk," they are actually experimenting with all of the sounds represented in all languages. As they learn a specific language, they become more proficient in the sounds of that language and forget how to make sounds that they don't need or use.

Phonetic Transcriptions and Terminology

There is controversy as to whether phonetic transcriptions should be used in the classroom, especially with younger learners. Regardless of one's position, phonetic transcriptions can be of value when diacritics are used to indicate the exact sounds a speaker of any language makes (narrow transcription).

PHONETIC TRANSCRIPTION draws on the total resources of the International Phonetic Alphabet (IPA) to mark minute distinctions in sound and which places symbols in square brackets. Accordingly a distinction would be made between the Spanish dental /t/ and the English /t/ of a more **ALVEOLAR** nature. These transcriptions are referred to as **NARROW TRANSCRIPTIONS** because of the specific information described and are used to distinguish between languages, accents, and individual speakers.

Phonemic transcription will be more likely encountered by teachers and their students in the classroom. Phonemic transcription is less exact than phonetic transcription, is generally well understood by students, and is more frequently

PHONOLOGY: the way in which speech sounds form patterns

Phonology is based on the theory that every native speaker unconsciously retains the sound structure of that language and is more concerned with the sounds than with the physical process of creating those sounds.

PHONETIC TRANSCRIPTION: marks minute distinctions in sound and places symbols in square brackets

ALVEOLAR: a speech sound that is made with the tip of the tongue touching the roof of the mouth near the front teeth

NARROW TRANSCRIPTIONS: transcriptions that are used to distinguish between languages, accents, and individual speakers encountered in textbooks. The transcriptions are made between diagonal slashes, i.e., / /. The following is an example of broad phonemic transcription:

Example: /paesm ə bodl əv waɪn n səm fɪʃnʧɪps/ or

"Pass them a bottle of wine and some fish and chips."

Place and Manner of Articulation

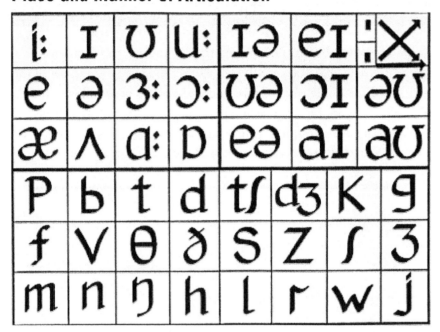

Underhill (1994) developed a phonemic chart to illustrate how the 44 English phonemes from the IPA chart are related to each other. The upper left-hand quadrant refers to vowels, and the upper right-hand quadrant to diphthongs. The bottom half of the chart refers to the consonants.

The chart below shows the interpretation of the consonant symbols.

Interpretation of the consonant symbols

p/	**p**it	/b/	**b**it
/t/	**t**in	/d/	**d**in
/k/	**c**ut	/g/	**g**ut
/tʃ/	**ch**eap	/dʒ/	**j**eep
/f/	**f**at	/v/	**v**at
/θ/	**th**in	/ð/	**th**en

/s/	**s**ap	/z/	**z**ap
/ʃ/	**sh**e	/ʒ/	mea**s**ure
/x/	lo**ch**		
/w/	**w**e	/m/	**m**ap
/l/	**l**eft	/n/	**n**ap
/ɹ/	**r**un (also /r/, /ɻ/)	/j/	**y**es
/h/	**h**am	/ŋ/	ba**ng**

The upper left quadrant of Underhill's chart, and the following table, present the
monophthong sounds or vowel sounds:

Monophthongs

IPA Symbol	Indicative word	Phonemic Transcription
i:	bee	/bi:/
ɪ	bit	/bɪt/
ʊ	wood	/wʊd/
u:	two	/tʊ;/
e	leg	/leg/
ə [called the 'schwa']	<u>a</u>way	/əweɪ/
ɜ:	her	/hɜ:/
ɔ	four	/fɔ:/
æ	cat	/cæt/
ʌ	up	/ʌp/
ɑ:	ask	/ɑ:sk/
ɒ	on	/ɒn/

Primary cardinal vowels

1	[i]	bean, team, seed
2	[e]	leg
3	[ɛ]	her
4	[ɑ]	ask, cat
5	[ɒ]	hot, cot, olive, bra

6	[ɔ]	four, caught
7	[o]	coat
8	[u]	two, coot

The upper right quadrant of Underhill's chart, and the following table, present the eight diphthong sounds:

Diphthongs

IPA Symbol	Indicative word	Phonemic Transcription
ɪə	here	/hɪə/
eɪ	eight	/eɪt/
ʊə	cure	/kjʊə/
ɔɪ	boy	/bɔɪ/
əʊ	no	/nəʊ/
eə	there	/ðeə/
aɪ	my	/maɪ/
aʊ	now	/naʊ/

The bottom half of Underhill's chart the consonant sector. The chart uses the three variables associated with English speech: voiced/voiceless, place of articulation, and manner of articulation.

- Voiced/voiceless: In the first two rows of the consonant half of the chart, notice that the sounds are paired, with the voiceless phoneme always on the left of the pair (i.e., P/b, t/d).

- Place of articulation: The pairing itself refers to place. The pairs /p/ and /b/ and /t/ and /d/ are bilabial and alveolar respectively, and so on. Note that these groupings are in the first two rows only.

- Manner of articulation: The first row is plosive, the second row fricative.

Phonemes, pitch, and stress are all components of phonology. Because each affects the meaning of communications, they are variables that English language learners (ELLs) must recognize and learn.

Phonology analyzes the sound structure of the given language by

- Determining which phonetic sounds have the most significance

- Explaining how these sounds influence a native speaker of the language

Mastering a sound that does not occur in the learner's first language requires ongoing repetition, both of hearing the sound and attempting to say it. The older the learner, the more difficult this becomes, especially if the learner has only spoken one language before reaching puberty. Correct pronunciation may literally require years of practice because initially the learner may not hear the sound correctly. Expecting an ELL to master a foreign pronunciation quickly leads to frustration for the teacher and the learner. With enough focused repetition, however, the learner may eventually hear the difference and then be able to imitate it. Inadequate listening and speaking practice will result in a persistent heavy accent.

PHONEMES are the smallest unit of sound that affects meaning, i.e., to distinguish two words. In English, there are approximately 44 speech sounds yet only 26 letters, so the sounds, when combined, become words. For this reason, English is not considered a phonetic language where there is a one-to-one correspondence between letters and sounds. For example, consider the two words, *pin* and *bin*. The only difference is the first consonant of the words, the /p/ in *pin* and /b/ in *bin*. This makes the sounds /p/ and /b/ phonemes in English, because the difference in sound creates a difference in meaning.

Focusing on phonemes to provide pronunciation practice allows students to have fun while they learn to recognize and say sounds. Pairs or groups of words that have a set pattern make learning easier. For example, students can practice saying or thinking of words that rhyme but begin with a different phoneme, such as *tan, man, fan,* and *ran*. Other groups of words might start with the same phoneme followed by various vowel sounds, such as *ten, ton, tan,* and *tin*. This kind of alliteration can be expanded into tongue twisters that students find challenging and fun.

Vowels and consonants should be introduced in a deliberate order to allow combinations that form real words, though made-up words that have no real meaning in English should also be encouraged when introducing new sounds.

Stress and Intonation Patterns

PITCH in communication determines the context or meaning of words or series of words. A string of words can communicate more than one meaning; for example, when posed as a question or statement. For example, the phrase "I can't go" acts as a statement. If the pitch or intonation rises for the word go, the same phrase becomes the question: "I can't go?"

STRESS can occur at a word or sentence level. At the word level, different stresses on the syllable can actually modify the word's meaning. Consider the word *conflict*. To pronounce it as a noun, one would stress the first syllable, as in *CONflict*. To use it as a verb, however, the second syllable would be stressed, as in *conFLICT*.

> *Mastering a sound that does not occur in the learner's first language requires ongoing repetition, both of hearing the sound and attempting to say it.*

> **PHONEMES:** the smallest unit of sound that affects meaning, i.e., to distinguish two words

> *In English, there are approximately 44 speech sounds yet only 26 letters, so the sounds, when combined, become words. For this reason, English is not considered a phonetic language where there is a one-to-one correspondence between letters and sounds.*

> **PITCH:** determines the context or meaning of words or series of words

> **STRESS:** can modify the meaning of words or sentences

Different dialects sometimes pronounce the same word differently, even though both pronunciations have the same meaning. For example, in some parts of the United States the word *insurance* is pronounced by stressing the second syllable, while in other parts of the country the first syllable is stressed.

At the sentence level, stress can also be used to vary the meaning. For example, consider the following questions and how the meaning changes, according to the stressed words:

- *He* did that? (Emphasis is on the person)

- He *did* that? (Emphasis is on the action)

- He did *that*? (Emphasis is on object of the action)

This type of meaning differentiation is difficult for most ELL students to grasp and requires innovative teaching, such as acting out the three different meanings. Since pitch and stress can change the meaning of a sentence completely, however, students must learn to recognize these differences. Not recognizing sarcasm or anger can cause students considerable problems in their academic and everyday endeavors.

Unlike languages such as Spanish or French, English has multiple pronunciations of vowels and consonants, which contributes to making it a difficult language to learn. While phonetic rules are critical to learning to read and write, in spite of there being numerous exceptions, they do little to assist listening and speaking skills.

- Phonographemics: Refers to the study of letters and letter combinations. Unlike most languages, in English one symbol can represent many phonemes. While some phonetic rules apply, English has numerous exceptions, which make it difficult to learn.

  In teaching English to speakers of other languages, the wide variation of phonemes represented by a single symbol must be taught and *drilled*. If it is difficult for native speakers to learn the English spelling system, it's a great leap for the foreign language learner. Graphemes should be introduced long after spoken English. Students must first begin to be able to speak and hear the language before they can be taught to spell it.

  The phonology of English is an important component of an ESOL program.

- Phonographemic: Differences between words of English are a common source of confusion and thus need to be taught explicitly with plenty of learning activities to enable learners to acquire them sufficiently. Some areas of focus for the ESOL classroom include:

  – Homonyms: A general term that describes word forms that have two or more meanings, i.e., can (to be able) and can (a container).

- Homographs: Two or more words that have the same spelling or pronunciation but different meanings, i.e., stalk (part of a plant) and stalk (to follow).

- Homophones: Two or more words that have the same pronunciation but different meanings and spelling, i.e., wood/would, cite/sight.

- Heteronyms: Two or more words that have the same spelling but have a different pronunciation and meaning, i.e., Polish/polish.

Generalities of United States English Pronunciation

General American (GA) English is considered to be the typical English pronunciation in the United States. GA excludes many recognizable regionalisms and specific social groups. It is used as a norm for national broadcasters. Origins of GA are in the Midwest region.

General American (or Standard American) English is **RHOTIC**, in other words, the /r/ is pronounced before a consonant and at the end of a word: *port, dear, curl*. However, there are a few non-rhotic accents in the United States, especially in urban working-class areas like New York, Boston, a few conservative dialects of the South, and Black English.

> **RHOTIC:** a dialect in which the /r/ is pronounced before a consonant and at the end of a word: *port, dear, curl.*

Most GA speakers use the same vowel sound /ɑ:/ for words such as *father* or *bother*. Many use the same vowel /ɑ:/ for *cot* or *caught*. In GA, the contrast between "short" vowels and "long" vowels is not as marked as in other varieties of English. GA has "short a" /æ/, in most words where /a/ is followed by either /n/ followed by another consonant (*plant*) or /s/ (*pass*), /f/ (*laugh*), or /θ/ (*path*).

General Terms to Know Concerning Phonology

TERM	DEFINITION	ILLUSTRATIVE EXAMPLE
Assimilation	Refers to a phoneme being spoken differently when it is near another phoneme	*And* /æ nd/ is usually spoken as /n/ in rapid, casual speech
Diphthong	A complex speech sound or *glide* that begins with one vowel and gradually changes to another vowel within the same syllable A	The /oi/ in *boil* or /ī/ in *fine* are English diphthongs

Continued on next page

Elision	Omission of a sound between two words (usually a vowel and the end of one word or the beginning of the next)	"John and Peter are going to the store" "…/ə gəʊɪŋ/…" In this case the verb are is elided to a mere schwa /ə/
Affricative (also called affricate)	A complex speech sound consisting of a stop consonant followed by a fricative	The initial sounds of child and joy are English affricates
Fricatives	A consonant characterized by frictional passage of the expired breath through a narrowing at some point in the vocal tract	The sounds /v/ /θ/ /ð/ /s/ /z/ /ʃ/ /ʒ/ and /h/ are English fricatives
Plosives	A stop or occlusive produced by stopping the airflow in the vocal tract	The sounds /p/, /t/, /k/, /b/, /d/, /g/ are English plosives
Reduction	Shortening pronunciation of words	wanna, gimme, or lemme
Laterals	/L/-like consonants sounds	clear /l/ as in lady, fly and the dark /l/ as in bold or tell
Linking Sounds	Sounds that are joined together, frequently a final consonant with an initial consonant or a vowel with an initial vowel by inserting a /w/ or /y/	turn off = turn off so I = soWI do all = doWall

The Effects of Phonetic Environment on Pronunciation

There are three major branches of phonetics, the science or study of sounds of speech:

- Articulatory phonetics: The oldest branch, which investigates the ways in which sounds are made.

- Acoustic phonetics: Studies speech as it is heard or its waveform. The waveform of consonants and vowels is presented as a spectrogram where sounds appear as recognizable patterns.

- Experimental phonetics: Usually concerns the manipulation of the waveform and tests to identify which aspects of sound are necessary for understanding.

Phonetics applications have been made in areas such as language teaching, speech therapy, and automatic speech synthesis and recognition. (See the *Oxford Companion to the English Language*, 1992).

More recent studies concentrate on the effect of phonetic environment on pronunciation. For example, Roeder (2009) challenges previously held studies of Stevens and House (1963) in which Stevens claims the speech of humans is "inherent to the dynamic properties of the articulatory structures and of the neuromuscular system that controls them." Her studies indicate that there are additional factors that influence the understanding and reproduction of speech other than the linguistic apparatus. Stevens (1998) briefly mentions that the overall variation in vowels can occur across regional dialects.

Language teachers are familiar with the difficulties in reproducing sounds such as the rolled /r/ or a guttural click when these sounds are not part of the student's native language. For similar reasons, Japanese students may have difficulty with the /l/ or /r/ and Spanish students with the short vowel sounds: *pet, pit, pot, put, putt.*

> **MORPHEME:** the smallest unit of language system that has meaning

> *These units are more commonly known as: the root word, the prefix and the suffix.*

SKILL 2.2 **Types of morphemes** *(e.g., stem/root and affix, bound and free, derivational and inflectional)* **and how words are morphologically related to each other**

A **MORPHEME** is the smallest unit of language system that has meaning. These units are more commonly known as: the root word, the prefix, and the suffix, and they cannot be broken down into any smaller units.

The **ROOT WORD OR BASE WORD** is the key to understanding a word, because this is where the actual meaning is determined.

A **PREFIX** acts as a syllable that appears in front of the root or base word and can alter the meaning of the root or base word.

A **SUFFIX** is a letter or letters that are added to the end of the word and can alter the original tense or meaning of the root or base word.

MORPHOLOGY refers to the process of how the words of a language are formed to create meaningful messages. Some underlying principles of the morphology of English are:

> **ROOT WORD OR BASE WORD:** where the actual meaning is determined

> **PREFIX:** appears in front of the root or base word and can alter its meaning

> **SUFFIX:** a letter or letters added to the end of the word; can alter the original tense or meaning of the root or base word

> **MORPHOLOGY:** the process of how the words of a language are formed to create meaningful messages

1. Morphemes may be free and able to stand by themselves (e.g., chair, bag) or they may be bound or derivational and need to be used with other morphemes to create meaning (e.g., read-able, en-able). The largest group of derivative suffixes are the nominalizers, which change adjectives or verbs into nouns (e.g., *acy, -ance, -ician, -ism, -ist, -ity, -ment, -ster, -able, -al, -an, -atic.*)

2. Knowledge of the meanings of derivational morphemes such as prefixes and suffixes enables students to decode word meanings and create words in the language through word analysis, e.g., *un-happy* means not happy.

3. An inflection is a grammatical form of the word. In English, all inflections are suffixes and occur at the very end of the word. English verbs are inflected for mood, tense, person, and number. Regular verbs inflect using suffixes while irregular verbs have past tense forms that are different from the normal inflection. Nouns and adjectives are inflected for plurality and possession (teacher/teachers; teacher's/teachers'). Some adjectives inflect for comparatives and superlatives (pretty/prettier/prettiest). Seven pronoun forms have different objective forms: me, us, her, him, them, thee, whom. (*Oxford Companion to the English Language*, 1992).

4. Morphologically, words are of two classes: grammatical words and lexical words. Examples of grammatical words are: of, the, and, which, but, so, some. Grammatical words are rarely borrowed from other languages or invented. Lexical words, on the other hand, are constantly being borrowed or invented. They are the content words that name objects, concepts, qualities, processes, events, and actions in the world. (Traugott and Pratt, 1980).

5. Words can be combined in English to create new compound words (e.g., key + chain = *keychain*).

MORPHEMIC ANALYSIS requires breaking a word down into its component parts to determine its meaning. It shows the relationship between the root or base word and the prefix and/or suffix to determine the word's meaning.

The following is an example of how morphemic analysis can be applied to a word:

- Choose a root or base word, such as *kind*.

- Create as many new words as possible by changing the prefix and suffix.

- New words, would include *unkind, kindness,* and *kindly*.

ESOL learners need to understand the structure of words in English and how words may be created and altered. Learning common roots, prefixes, and suffixes greatly helps ELLs to decode unfamiliar words. This can make a big difference in how well a student understands written language. Students who can decode unfamiliar words become less frustrated when reading in English and, as a result,

MORPHEMIC ANALYSIS: the process of breaking a word down into its component parts to determine its meaning

Knowledge of the meanings of derivational morphemes such as prefixes and suffixes enables students to decode word meanings and create words in the language through word analysis.

In English, all inflections are suffixes and occur at the very end of the word.

are likely to read more. They have greater comprehension and their language skills improve more quickly. Having the tools to decode unfamiliar words enables ELLs to perform better on standardized tests because they are more likely to understand the questions and answer choices.

ESOL teachers need to be aware of the principles of morphology in English to provide meaningful activities that will help in the process of language acquisition.

Guessing at the meaning of words should be encouraged. Too often students become dependent on translation dictionaries, which cause the students not to develop morphemic analysis skills. Practice should include identifying roots, prefixes, and suffixes, as well as using morphemic knowledge to form new words.

ESOL teachers also need to be aware that principles of morphology from the native language may be transferred to either promote or interfere with the second language learning process.

SKILL 2.3 **English syntax** *(e.g., how words are combined into phrases and sentences, and transformations such as question formation)*, **the parts of speech, and the tenses of English verbs**

The English Syntactic System

English classifies eight parts of speech, each with a specific role in sentences. Understanding the parts of speech can be quite difficult for ELLs because the same word can have a different role in different sentences, and a different meaning entirely. Identifying the subject and predicate of the sentence helps to distinguish what role a particular word plays in a sentence. Since English is an subject-verb-object (S-V-O) language, the placement of a word in a sentence relative to the subject or verb indicates what part of speech it is.

- That TV *show* was boring.

- I will *show* you my new dress.

- The band plays *show* tunes at half time.

> *Too often students become dependent on translation dictionaries, which cause the students not to develop morphemic analysis skills.*

> *ESOL teachers also need to be aware that principles of morphology from the native language may be transferred to either promote or interfere with the second language learning process.*

In these examples, the word show is first a noun, then a verb, and finally an adjective.

THE EIGHT PARTS OF SPEECH	
Noun	A person, place, thing or idea. Common nouns are non-specific, while proper nouns name a particular person, place, thing, or idea, and are capitalized.
	Nouns may be countable or uncountable. Countable nouns describe countable objects, e.g., an apple, twelve chairs, six geese, a cup of coffee. Uncountable nouns describe things that cannot be counted, e.g., liberty, coffee, or politics. *Many* and *few* are used when referring to countable nouns, and *much* and *little* when referring to uncountable nouns.
Verb	An action or state of being.
Pronoun	A word that takes the place of a noun. A pronoun refers back to the word it replaces—its antecedent.
	There are three types of pronouns:
	• **Personal pronouns** can be
	– first, second, or third person (I, you, he, she it)
	– singular or plural (I/we, you/you, he, she, it/they)
	– subjective or objective (I/me, you/you, he/him, she/her, it/it, we/us, they/them)
	• **Possessive pronouns** show ownership (my, mine, your, yours, his, her, hers, its, our, ours, your, yours, their, and theirs).
	• **Indefinite pronouns** refer to persons, places, things or ideas in general, e.g., any, each, both, most, something.
Adjective	A word that modifies a noun or pronoun. Adjectives answer the questions, *What kind? How many?* and *Which?*
Adverb	A word that modifies a verb, an adjective, or another adverb. Adverbs answer the questions, *How? When? Where? How often?* and *To what extent?*

Continued on next page

Preposition	A word that, in a phrase with a noun or pronoun, shows the relationship between a noun or pronoun and another word in a sentence. Prepositions describe or show location, direction, or time. Prepositional phrases can have as few as two words, but can include any number of adjectives.
Interjection	A word that shows surprise or strong feeling. An interjection can stand alone (*Help!*) or be used within a sentence (*Oh no, I forgot my wallet!*)

Conjunction	Conjunctions may be either coordinating or subordinating.
	
	 • Coordinating conjunctions (*and, but, or, nor*) connect words or phrases that have the same grammatical function in a sentence. The coordinating conjunction pair *either/or* is used for affirmative statements; the pair *neither/nor* is used for negative statements.
	
	 Parallel structure is desired when using coordinating conjunctions, e.g., *to ride, to sing,* and *to dance.* (Similar structures for clauses are indicated.) The coordinating conjunctions (*so, for, yet*) may also be used to connect two independent clauses.
	
	 • Subordinating conjunctions are words used to introduce adverbial clauses. Some* of the subordinating conjunctions used for _____ are:
	
	   — **time:** *after, before, when, while, as, as soon as, since, until*
	
	   — **cause and effect:** *because, now that, since*
	
	   — **contrast:** *although, even though, though*
	
	   — **condition:** *if, only if, unless, whether or not, in that case,* e.g., "When we were in Brazil, we went to Rio de Janeiro and Sao Paulo." "We went to Rio de Janeiro and Sao Paulo when we were in Brazil."

(*There are many, many more subordinating conjunctions.)

Sentences

A sentence is a group of words that has a subject and predicate, and expresses a complete idea. A subject tells us what or whom the sentence is about and the predicate makes a statement about what the subject is or does. (In all the following examples, subjects are underlined and predicates italicized.)

PARTS OF A SAMPLE SENTENCE	
Example sentence: <u>The snow</u> *falls quietly*	
Subject	The subject, or the topic of a sentence, consists of a noun or a pronoun and all the words that modify it. "The snow" is the subject in the above example. The simple subject is the main part of the subject. <u>Snow</u> is the simple subject.
Predicate	The predicate makes a statement or a comment about the subject and it consists of a verb and all the words that modify it; *falls quietly* is the predicate in the above example. The simple predicate is the main part of the predicate and is always the verb; <u>falls</u> is the simple predicate.
Compound subject	A subject that consists of two or more nouns or pronouns, e.g., <u>Books and magazines</u> *filled the room.*
Compound predicate	A predicate that contains more than one verb pertaining to the subject, e.g., <u>The boys</u> *walked and talked.*

Sentence types

Subjects and predicates can be modified and combined in different ways to make simple, compound, or complex sentences.

SENTENCE TYPES	
Simple	A simple sentence, or independent clause, is a complete thought consisting of a subject and a predicate: <u>The bus</u> *was late.*
Compound	A compound sentence consists of two independent clauses joined together by a coordinator (*and, or, nor, but, for, yet, so*): <u>Tom</u> *walked to the bus station,* **and** <u>he</u> *took the bus.*
Complex	A complex sentence is a sentence consisting of a dependent clause (a group of words with a subject and predicate that are not a complete thought) and an independent clause joined together using a subordinator (*although, after, when, because, since, while*): <u>After I</u> *write the report,* <u>I</u> *will submit it to my teacher.*

Sentence purposes

Sentences serve different purposes. They can make a statement (declarative); ask a question (interrogative); give a command (imperative); or express a sense of urgency (exclamatory). Understanding the different purposes for sentences can help ELLs understand the relationship between what they write and the ideas they want to express.

SENTENCE PURPOSE	
Declarative	A declarative sentence makes a statement: "Anna will feed the dog."
Interrogative	An interrogative sentence asks a question: "Anna, have you fed the dog?"
Imperative	An imperative sentence gives a command: "Anna, please feed the dog."
Exclamatory	An exclamatory sentence expresses a sense of urgency: "Anna, go feed the dog right now!"

Constructing sentences involves combining words in grammatically correct ways to communicate the desired thought. Avoiding fragments and run-ons requires continual sentence analysis. The test of a complete sentence is: Does it contain a subject and predicate and express a complete idea?

ELLs often overgeneralize that sentence fragments are short and complete sentences are long. When they truly understand what constitutes a sentence, they will realize that length has nothing to do with whether a sentence is complete or not. For example:

- *"He ran." is a complete sentence.*
- *"After the very funny story began" is a fragment.*

To make these distinctions, learners must know the parts of speech and understand the difference between independent clauses and dependent clauses. Practice identifying independent clauses, dependent clauses, and phrases will help ELLs to write complete sentences.

CLAUSES AND PHRASES	
Independent Clause	Independent clauses can stand alone or can be joined to other clauses.
Dependent Clause	Dependent clauses contain at least one subject and one verb, but they cannot stand alone as a complete sentence. They are structurally dependent on the main clause.

Continued on next page

Phrase	A phrase is a group of words that does not have a subject and a predicate and cannot stand alone. The most common types of phrases are: • Prepositional: "in the room" • Participial: "walking down the street" • Infinitive: "to run"

Sentence transformations

Sentences are transformed to add, delete, or permute informational content. There are many kinds of grammar. Chomsky proposed transformational grammar beginning in the 1950s. The term is still used to explain the relationships between the spoken word and its underlying meaning by distinguishing between sounds, words (and word parts), groups of words, and phrases. Sentences have a surface structure and an underlying structure according to generative grammarians. The rules that interpret the underlying structures and modify them to create the same surface structure are called **TRANSFORMATIONS**.

TRANSFORMATIONS: the rules that interpret the underlying structures and modify them to create the same surface structure

There are numerous possible transformations in the English language. Some of the most common ones used in ESOL teaching are listed below.

SENTENCE TRANSFORMATIONS: WAYS IN WHICH THE SENTENCE ADDS, DELETES, OR PERMUTES COMPONENTS	
Yes/No Questions	Sentences may be transformed into yes/no questions. **auxiliary verb + subject + main verb + rest of sentence:** He lives in Chicago. Does he live in Chicago? Yes, he does. No, he doesn't.
Information Questions	Sentences may be transformed into information questions. **question word + auxiliary verb + subject + main verb + rest of sentence:** Susan lives near Orlando. Where does Susan live? Near Orlando./She lives near Orlando. Will Julius be living alone in the house? How will Julius be living in the house? Alone./Julius will be living alone in the house.

Continued on next page

Active Voice to Passive Voice or Vice Versa	Sentences may be changed from one voice to another voice. I saw John. John was seen by me. John was being helped by me. I was helping John.
Indirect Objects	The word "to" (phrase marker) may be deleted. I gave a cookie to him. I gave him a cookie. I mailed the article to the newspaper. I mailed the newspaper the article.
Imperatives	The imperative or commands have no expressed subject. You sit. You jump. Sit! Jump!
Negatives	Linguists distinguish between two types of negation **Affirmative sentences may be transformed into negative sentences where the whole sentence is negative.** Marion is happy. Marion is not happy. **Parts of sentences may be negative.** Juliana is happy. Juliana is unhappy.

Verb tense

The basic English verb tenses are itemized below. Tense refers to any conjugated form expressing time, aspect, or mood. The charts omit the negative and interrogative forms.

VERB TENSES	SIMPLE	PROGRESSIVE	PERFECT	PERFECT PROGRESSIVE
Present	I write	I am writing	I have written	I have been writing
Past	I wrote	I was writing	I had written	I had been writing
Future	I will write	I will be writing	I will have written	I will have been writing

This table, of course, omits a number of forms that can be regarded as additional to the basic system:

- The intensive present: *I do write*

- The intensive past: *I did write*

- The habitual past: *I used to write*

- The "shall future": *I shall write*

- The "going-to future": *I am going to write*

- The "future in the past": *I was going to write*

- The conditional: *I would write*

- The perfect conditional: *I would have written*

- The subjunctive: *if I be writing, if I were writing*

SKILL 2.4 Basic features of semantics and how combinations of words convey meaning (e.g., phrases, sentences, and idioms)

> **SEMANTICS:** the branch of linguistics concerned with meaning

SEMANTICS is the branch of linguistics concerned with meaning. Modern semantics is largely derived from the work of the Swiss linguist Ferdinand de Saussure. In the most ample sense, semantics is concerned with the relations within a language (sense) and relations between language and the world (reference). Structural or lexical semantics concerns the sense relations associated with a word (lexical item/lexeme) and with a lexical structure. Reference studies the meaning of words, sentences, etc., in terms of the world of experience, or rather, the situations to which they refer or in which they occur (*Oxford Companion to the English Language*, 1992).

> Semantics is concerned with the relations within a language (sense) and relations between language and the world (reference).

> The "literal" meaning of a sentence is determined by the grammatical and lexical components and is unaffected by the context or what the speaker "meant" to say.

The meaning of a sentence (or phrase) is usually assumed to be derived from the words in the sentence, but meaning is often derived from the whole sentence and its context. Lyons (1977) distinguished between sentence meaning as determined by sentence meaning and utterance meaning. The "literal" meaning of a sentence is determined by the grammatical and lexical components and is unaffected by the context or what the speaker "meant" to say.

UTTERANCES		
Presupposition	Speech that is not spoken, but nevertheless, understood by the speaker.	The Headquarters of the American Orchid Society of America is located in Delray Beach, Florida. (The sentence presupposes that there is an American Orchid Society.)
Implication (associated with H.P. Grice)	Concerns implications the listener can make from utterances without actually being told. It includes presupposition.	I tried to send an email to the director. (Implies that for some reason I was unsuccessful.)
Prosodic Features	Use of stress and tone to convey meaning.	Jonathan visited *Miriam*. (Suggests Jonathan visited Miriam and no one else). Jonathan *visited* Miriam. (Suggests Jonathan visited Miriam, but did not call, email, or text her.)
Speech acts (associated with J.L. Austin. *How to Do Things with Words*, 1962)	Utterances (goal-directed actions) whose purpose is to get people to do things, contractual speech acts such as promising, betting, agreeing on a plan, and describing, informing, explaining, criticizing, judging and evaluating.	I christen the child Elizabeth Michelle Jones. (The utterance is not a statement of fact, but an action.) I declare the XXV Winter Olympics closed. (The act of closing the games.) Can you pass the potatoes? (This question is actually a request to perform the action.)

Idioms

Idioms cause much grief for ELLs because their meaning is figurative and not literal. The literal interpretation of most idioms is senseless and causes confusion to those studying a new language.

The best approach to learning idioms is to study them as they come up in reading, conversation, or instruction. Students may wish to compose a book of the literal meaning and the figurative meaning. Another option is to avail oneself of the Internet site *www.idiomconnection.com*, which lists idioms alphabetically and by topic. There is also a list of the 80 most frequently used idioms.

Examples:
• *"Ball is in (someone's court)": It is the decision of another person or group to do something. The ball is in the President's court after the mid-term elections.*
• *"Back to basics": An educational approach that uses successful traditional ideas or methods. The ESOL teacher used a back-to-basics approach in teaching the science content to her ELL students.*

SKILL 2.5   **Familiarity with differences among languages in terms of their phonology, morphology, syntax, and semantics**

Languages have many similarities. Linguists have tried to explain this by saying that the constraints in language are genetic; others claim we perceive dualities much more easily than three-part structures; and still others claim that the constraints are explicable in terms of language functions (Traugott and Pratt, 1980).

Yet, languages are very different. In distinct languages, different sounds are used to construct meaning. All spoken languages have phonemes: vowels and consonants. English for example has 26 letters broken down into19 consonants and 5 vowels; the letters /w/ and /y/ are sometimes used as consonants and at other times, as vowels. These letters are used to represent 44 different phonemes of English. Spanish has 29 letters, three more than English including /ch/, /ll/, and /ñ/. The modern Russian alphabet is a variation of the Cyrillic alphabet and contains 33 letters.

The way a speaker uses *pitch* can convey different meanings of the same word. In languages such as Chinese, Burmese, and Yoruba, word meanings are determined by pitch. English is not a tone language, but sentence meaning may be determined by pitch. For example, *yes* may mean different things depending on whether:

- The voice is rising = a question
- The voice is falling = agreement
- The voice is neutral = agreement with reservation
- The voice falls abruptly = annoyance
- The voice falls slightly and then rises = querulousness

The morphology of languages can be distinctive. All inflections in English are suffixes occurring at the end of a word. However, when signaling the future tense in English, a separate verb must be used: e.g., "He <u>will</u> leave after the party." This is not true of French or Spanish where the inflection is attached to the verb. Latin, Greek, and Russian require gender, number, and case inflections on the nouns.

The syntax of languages is distinctive. Observe that the sentence structure in Modern English, Yoruba, and Thai is the same: "I saw them." In Old English and Japanese, however, the structure is "I them saw." Hebrew and Welsh favor: "Saw I them." (Traugott and Pratt, 1980).

The semantics of languages are unique. Lexical semantics refers to the "word", particularly to the sense of the word, while sentence semantics refers to the meanings between different parts of the sentence. At the word level, *strawberry* is a plant, a fruit, and even a color. In the following sentence, "The girl ate the strawberry," *strawberry* is the receiver of the action level. In the next example, "Strawberry colored the room," *strawberry* is used as the agent of the action.

Different languages have different ways of expressing ideas or thoughts that are unique to their world or reference. The Inuits in Alaska have two root words to express snow, but add numerous affixes to them to describe snow depending on its condition, color, location, etc. In Russian, the color *blue* is considered generally to be either "light blue" or "dark blue," but not just blue. In Spanish, the faucets are either "opened" or "shut," but one cannot "turn the faucet on" or "turn the faucet off" as in English. These are just a few of the numerous differences linguists encounter when comparing or studying different languages.

COMPETENCY 3
LANGUAGE IN CULTURE

SKILL 3.1 **Basic concepts of pragmatics and sociolinguistics** *(i.e., that language varies according to a speaker's identity, purpose, and context)*

SOCIOLINGUISTICS is the study of how social conditions influence the use of language.

Social factors such as ethnicity, religion, gender, status, age, and education all play a role in how individuals use language. Different dialects or "how language is spoken" differ depending on these and other factors. Sociolinguistics tries to understand the relationship between language and the social elements.

Beyond anyone's control, language is constantly changing. In the words of H. L. Mencken, "A living language is like a man suffering incessantly from small hemorrhages, and what it needs above all else is constant transactions of new blood from other tongues. The day the gates go up, that day it begins to die."

Wars have added words to our language. During World War II, people began to use words such as *flak, blitz, R and R, black market, pin-up, mushroom cloud,* and *fallout.* During the Korean War, *chopper* and *brainwashing* came into use. During

SOCIOLINGUISTICS: the study of how social conditions influence the use of language

Social factors such as ethnicity, religion, gender, status, age, and education all play a role in how individuals use language.

A living language is like a man suffering incessantly from small hemorrhages, and what it needs above all else is constant transactions of new blood from other tongues. The day the gates go up, that day it begins to die.

—H. L. Mencken

the Vietnam era, *napalm, friendly fire, search-and-destroy mission*, and the *domino theory* entered the language. The Iraq War has added *the green zone, Al Qaeda*, and *weapons of mass destruction*. Wars also give new meanings to old words, such as *embedded*, which in the context of Iraq means journalists who join army units.

Contemporary culture changes language significantly. Advertisers have such great success that brand names come to represent entire categories of products, such as *Kleenex* for tissue; *Xerox* for photocopy; Hoover for vacuum cleaner; and *Coke* for cola. People pick up and use phrases from popular TV shows: *Yabadabadoo; like, cool, man; go go gadget; meathead;* and *d'oh!* Other cultural trends, such as the drug culture, sports, and fads add new words to the language.

Political rhetoric also influences language. We hear sports metaphors (a success referred to as a home run); war metaphors (victories or defeats); and business metaphors (ending up in the red or the black). Politicians like to "send a message" to enemies, political rivals, or the American people. Candidates like to be "the candidate of change" or "the education candidate."

Technology and science may have changed language more than any other factor in the past century. An estimated 500,000 technical and scientific terms have been added to English. Many of these words affect our daily lives. Fifty years ago, people didn't routinely use computers, cell phones, the Internet, or satellite dishes. They hadn't had an MRI and hadn't wondered if GMOs were safe to eat.

Text messaging, particularly among young people, has created a kind of shorthand variation of English: *CUL8R* means "see you later"; *BRB* means "be right back"; and *TTYL* means "talk to you later." ESL teachers might be surprised at how adroit their students are with technological language. Students who make English-speaking friends and want to adapt to American culture will quickly learn this new language.

The merging of languages into English has contributed to the inconsistencies and exceptions to rules that make the language difficult to learn. It has also increased the number of words one must learn to communicate in English. We can only be certain that English will continue to change, and language will continue to be vital in new forms.

Pragmatics is the study of how context impacts the interpretation of language. Situations dictate language choice, body language, degree of intimacy, and how meaning is interpreted.

PRAGMATICS: the study of how context impacts the interpretation of language; situations dictate language choice, body language, degree of intimacy, and how meaning is interpreted

PRAGMATICS involves the use of language and how speakers of a language use rules to govern the interactions between different speakers. A speaker's "communicative competence" is a speaker's knowledge of how to use language to communicate with others and how to understand their utterances. Thus, pragmatics is the study of how context impacts the interpretation of language. Situations dictate language choice, body language, degree of intimacy, and how meaning is interpreted.

For example, when customers walk into a bar and sit down on a stool, they expect a bartender will ask them several questions: "What would you like to drink?" and "Would you like to start a tab?" This sequence of events and cues is a typical pattern of interaction in a bar. Pragmatic knowledge provides the customer with a set of expectations for the flow of events. Pragmatic knowledge sets customer expectations. Typically people in a bar expect a certain level of social exchange that allows congeniality without intrusiveness. They expect to receive a certain level of service and to use a particular level of manners. These types of exchanges are fairly universal in bars but would be completely inappropriate in a more formal setting, for example, such as conversing with the president of a corporation.

Gestures, the appropriate distance between speakers, seating arrangements, nodding or shaking of the head, signs, and touch are all examples of nonverbal pragmatic conventions. These elements are different in different cultures and can be taught.

> Gestures, the appropriate distance between speakers, seating arrangements, nodding or shaking of the head, signs, and touch are all examples of nonverbal pragmatic conventions.

In the ESL classroom, pragmatics can be illustrated and practiced by repeating the same situation in different contexts. For example, students can write or act out how they would explain to three different people why they failed a test: their best friend, their teacher, and their parent. With a little imagination, different scenarios can be chosen that pique student interest and make learning fun. For example, explain an embarrassing event in different contexts, such as in front of a boy/girl you want to impress, a close friend, and an authority figure. For students with very low language skills, pantomime can encourage participation, teach the concept, and set up an opportunity for using language to describe what has happened.

SKILL 3.2 Understanding the nature and value of World Englishes and dialect variation, and communicative competence

The term, WORLD ENGLISH, became popular in the 1960s and increasingly has become a way to refer to English, which dominates many aspects of the political and economic progress of the world. World Englishes are considered to be American English, British English, Indian English, South African English, Japanese English and, according to many, the English used by other peoples to communicate in world trade, travel, and politics. Sometimes, this makes it difficult for teachers to decide which English to teach. However, since conservative estimates suggest that non-native English speakers outnumber native speakers, the question "Who's English are we talking about?" becomes a very important question in the ESOL classroom.

> **WORLD ENGLISH:** a term increasingly used to refer to English, which dominates many aspects of the political and economic progress of the world

Since conservative estimates suggest that non-native English speakers outnumber native speakers, the question "Who's English are we talking about?" becomes a very important question in the ESOL classroom.

The English-speaking world has been described by the Indian linguist Braj Kachru as containing three circles: the inner circle, the outer circle, and the expanding circle. In the inner circle are the traditional English-speaking countries such as the United Kingdom, the United States, Ireland, New Zealand, Australia, and Canada. The outer circle is composed of countries that are ex-colonies and that continue to have close ties with the U.K. and the U.S.: India, Malaysia, Singapore, the Philippines, and many African countries. The expanding circle includes all other countries of the world where English is being learned for reasons of information technology, travel, work, etc. These countries include South America, China, and Spain among others.

DIALECT VARIATION: a general and technical term for a form of a language

DIALECT VARIATION is a general and technical term for a form of a language: a southern French dialect; the Yorkshire dialect; or the dialects of the United States. Although the term generally refers to regional speech, it can be used to indicate class and occupation: a regional dialect, a rural dialect, a class dialect, or an occupational dialect. (McArthur, 1992).

Standard languages tend to develop among the officials of a country and the educated. They are considered to be non-regional or supra-regional, but not as dialects per se.

Dialects are prevalent in most languages. They have their distinctive accent, grammar, vocabulary, and idioms. In general, dialects have been considered inferior to the "standard" form of a language, such as the King's or Queen's English or Standard American English. Standard languages tend to develop among the officials of a country and the educated. They are considered to be non-regional or supra-regional, but not as dialects *per se*. Many users of Standard English tend to look down on those who speak dialects as "low," "vulgar," or "illiterate" (McArthur, 1992).

Communicative competence then becomes a highly subjective factor in the speech of ESOL students. Dell Hymes introduced the term in the 1970s. In broad terms, English language learners are expected to know grammar (in its most ample sense, including phonology, orthography, syntax, lexicon, and semantics) and the rules for its use in socially appropriate circumstances. (McArthur, 1992). Given the high-stakes testing of recent years, teachers and school officials are constantly working to improve communicative competence in their charges while making the process as painless and quick as possible.

SKILL 3.3 Range of social and academic language functions required for English-language proficiency

ELLs are generally expected to be proficient in four skill areas: listening, speaking, reading, and writing. Listening and reading are receptive skills while speaking and writing are productive skills. The National Council of Teachers of English and the International Reading Association (1996) proposed two new areas (viewing and visually representing) to reflect the growing importance of visual literacy. (Tompkins, 2009)

The following is a brief overview of the skills an ELL student might be expected to use to demonstrate English language proficiency.

ENGLISH LANGUAGE PROFICIENCY SKILLS	
LISTENING	• Listen to stories • Listen for information • Monitor their listening
SPEAKING	• Participate in discussions of literature • Give oral reports • Participate in debates • Participate in drama, role plays, and skit
READING	• Independent reading • Shared reading • Guided reading • Buddy reading • Reading aloud to children Read for different purposes Read for comprehension

Continued on next page

WRITING	Demonstrate spelling and handwriting proficiency
	Demonstrate the use of the writing process
	• Prewriting
	• Drafting
	• Revising
	• Editing
	• Publishing
	Experiment with different genres
	Experiment with informal writing when possible
VIEWING	(Includes film, videos, print advertisements, commercials, photographs, book illustrations, the Internet, and DVDs)
	• Use comprehension strategies similar to those used in reading
	• Use the Internet as a learning tool
	• Learn about propaganda
VISUALLY REPRESENTING	• Consider audience, purpose, and form when creating visual texts
	• Use visual texts to share information learned in class

(Adapted from Tompkins, 2009)

COMPETENCY 4
SECOND-LANGUAGE LEARNING

SKILL 4.1 Familiarity with research-based models for second language learning and acquisition *(e.g., cognitive, behaviorist, constructivist)*

The **COGNITIVE** (nativist/mentalist) **THEORY OF** second **LANGUAGE LEARNING** emphasizes the internal factors in children's language learning ability. Its supporters believe that a child learns a language in the same way as he learns other biological functions.

Chomsky (1959) theorized that the Language Acquisition Device (LAD) is an innate part of a child's inherited human character allowing infants to construct and internalize the grammar of their native language based on the limited and fragmented language input they receive. By using the LAD, children receive messages, form hypothesis based on the linguistic information they receive, and test out their hypothesis in speech and texts (Palacios and Arzamendi, 2005).

The **BEHAVIORIST THEORY OF LANGUAGE LEARNING** was largely based on the work of B.F. Skinner (1957). Skinner claimed that children entered the world as a blank slate and then are influenced by their environment. He coined the phrase "operant conditioning" to explain the stimulus-response actions. Emphasis of the behaviorists was on input.

In response to the behaviorist and cognitive theories of language learning, the American linguist Bloom (and Piaget, Bruner, Slobin, Halliday, and others) led the way to the **FUNCTIONAL, DEVELOPMENTAL,** or **INTERACTIONIST THEORY OF LANGUAGE LEARNING.** Piaget explains children's language development as an interaction with their environment, and at the same time, interaction between their perceptual cognitive capacities and their linguistic experiences. The interactionist theories argued that the interaction between the internal forces and input was the key factor in language learning.

Thus, **CONSTRUCTIVISTS** theorize that people construct their own meaning and knowledge of the world through experience and reflection on these experiences. New knowledge must be reconciled with previous knowledge (or discarded). As we ask questions, explore and assess what we know, knowledge is created. As the child is constantly exploring his world, he finds his knowledge of the world gaining in complexity and power.

> **COGNITIVE THEORY OF LANGUAGE LEARNING:** holds that a child learns a language in the same way as he learns other biological functions

> **BEHAVIORIST THEORY OF LANGUAGE LEARNING:** claims that children enter the world as a blank slate and then are influenced by their environment

> **FUNCTIONAL, DEVELOPMENTAL, OR INTERACTIONIST THEORY OF LANGUAGE LEARNING:** explains children's language development as an interaction with their environment, and at the same time, interaction between their perceptual cognitive capacities and their linguistic experiences

---

SKILL 4.2 Second-language acquisition, first-language acquisition, and how learners' first language can affect their second-language productions (e.g., L1 interference, accent, code switching)

Basic Principles and Theory Related to Second Language Acquisition

COMPREHENSION-BASED APPROACHES (CBA) or **COMPREHENSION-BASED LEARNING (CBL):** CBA/CBL language-acquisition approaches are focused on building up the learner's receptiveness for learning listening skills as well as some reading skills. The case for using a CBL or CBA approach is the following: sending and receiving information require different mental processing since speaking

> **COMPREHENSION-BASED APPROACHES (CBA) OR COMPREHENSION-BASED LEARNING (CBL):** language-acquisition approaches are focused on building up the learner's receptiveness for learning listening skills as well as some reading skills

is much more complex than listening. Therefore, placing extreme emphasis on speaking, when learning a second language, is counterproductive to positive second language acquisition (Celce-Murcia, 1991).

TOTAL PHYSICAL RESPONSE (TPR): J. Asher developed this CBA-based approach in the 1960s. The main premise underlying TPR is that children begin to learn when situations require them to give a meaningful action response, rather than a verbal one. The TPR approach is not as demanding or intimidating because it allows the learner to casually acquire the basic comprehensive skills needed to acquire future L2 proficiency (Celce-Murcia, 1991).

DELAYED ORAL RESPONSE (DOR): DOR is a CBA/CBL-based approach based on listening and visualization developed by V.A. Postovsky. He created a test program for instructing Russian through problem-solving tasks and multiple-choice answers. The learner was presented with four pictures on a screen, while listening to the problem in Russian. The learner responded by touching one of the four pictures. If the correct picture was selected, then the program went to the next task. If the program did not go to the next task, then the learner knew that she had to try again (Celce-Murcia, 1991).

OPTIMAL HABIT REINFORCEMENT (OHR): H. Winitz, a professor of speech science and psychology at the University of Missouri, experimented with OHR and created a self-instructional program, with audio cassettes and accompanying book, based on the principles of CBA/CBL. The self-instructional audio cassettes and book, called *The Learnables*, provided no feedback to the learners. The learning was very self-directed; if the learner decided that she did not understand the script corresponding to the picture in the book, then the learner just rewound the tape (Celce-Murcia, 1991).

NATURAL APPROACH: T. Terrell and S. Krashen are the researchers behind the most comprehensive CBA/CBL approach: the Natural Approach. The underlying assumption is that any learner of any age has the ability to receive comprehensible speech input and determine its pattern, without someone else having to spell it out for them. According to Terrell and Krashen, the approach involves large amounts of comprehensible input, whether it is situational, from visual aids/cues, or grammatical. This input is "respectful" of "the initial preproduction period, expecting speech to emerge not from artificial practice, but from motivated language use, progressing from early single-word responses up to more and more coherent discourse" (Celce-Murcia, 1991). Terrell also maintains that being "grammatically correct" is not as important as the learner's enjoying the learning process. Critics of Terrell maintain that by not correcting the learner's errors early on, fluency is achieved at the expense of accuracy.

TOTAL PHYSICAL RESPONSE (TPR): holds that children begin to learn when situations require them to give a meaningful action response

DELAYED ORAL RESPONSE (DOR): a CBA/CBL-based approach, created to instruct Russian through problem-solving tasks and multiple-choice answers

OPTIMAL HABIT REINFORCEMENT (OHR): a self-instructional program based on CBA/CBL principles, which provided no feedback to the learners

NATURAL APPROACH: assumes that any learner of any age has the ability to receive comprehensible speech input and determine its pattern, without someone else having to spell it out for them

SILENT WAY LEARNING (SWL): This strategy, pioneered by Caleb Gattegno, requires that the instructor, not the learner, remain quiet while trying to elicit input from the learners. The instructor may use visual aids/cues, gestures, etc., to give hints to the learners. The actual learning occurs when the learners attempt to speak, testing speaking skills related to meaning, form, and function. It is entirely up to the learner to decide what she will say, as well as which level of speech to use. "The cardinal principle the teacher must follow is phrased in four words: Subordinate teaching to learning" (Celce-Murcia, 1991).

NOTIONAL/FUNCTIONAL: Wilkins (1976) developed a system of language learning based on the "notions" (concepts such as location, frequency, time, sequence, etc.) and "functions" (requests, threats, complaints, offers, etc.) based on the system of meanings a learner would need to know in order to communicate. His "notional/functional" syllabus did not emphasize grammatical correctness but accuracy was implicit in the structures students practiced.

LEXICAL: Lewis (1993, 1997) proposed the idea of "chunks" of language that the learner must master to be able to communicate, thus firmly placing lexis back at the center of the language learning process. By learning fixed chunks (How do you do?) and semi-fixed chunks (According to the author/writer/editor, the main/principal/most interesting point to be seen is…), the ELL can greatly increase his language abilities.

COMMUNICATIVE COMPETENCE: Prabhu (1983) believes that language is acquired through meaning. The mental act of reasoning creates the conditions for learning, and tasks are an effective way of achieving learning in the language classroom, which he classified into three categories:

- Information-gap activities: Information is transferred from one person to another, one form to another, or one place to another.

- Reasoning activities: Implies the discovery through reasoning, inference, deduction, or a perception of patterns.

- Opinion-gap activities: Identification and expression of personal preferences or attitude in response to a situation.

SILENT WAY LEARNING (SWL): a strategy that requires that the instructor, not the learner, remain quiet; the actual learning occurs when the learner attempts to speak, testing speaking skills related to meaning, form, and function

NOTIONAL/FUNCTIONAL: a system of language learning based on the system of meanings a learner would need to know in order to communicate

LEXICAL: proposed the idea of "chunks" of language that the learner must master to be able to communicate, thus firmly placing lexis back at the center of the language learning process

COMMUNICATIVE COMPETENCE: holds that the mental act of reasoning creates the conditions for learning, and tasks are an effective way of achieving learning in the language classroom

PATTERNS IN SECOND-LANGUAGE DEVELOPMENT	
Silent Period	The stage when a learner knows perhaps 500 receptive words but feels uncomfortable producing speech. The absence of speech does not indicate a lack of learning, and teachers should not try to force the learner to speak. Comprehension can be checked by having the learner point or mime. Also known as the *Receptive or Preproduction stage*.
Private Speech	When the learner knows about 1,000 receptive words and speaks in one- or two-word phrases. The learner can use simple responses, such as yes/no, either/or. Also known as the *Early Production stage*.
Lexical Chunks	The learner knows about 3,000 receptive words and can communicate using short phrases and sentences. Long sentences typically have grammatical errors. Also known as the *Speech Emergence stage*.
Formulaic Speech	The learner knows about 6,000 receptive words and begins to make complex statements, state opinions, ask for clarification, share thoughts, and speak at greater length. Also known as the *Intermediate Language Proficiency stage*.
Experimental or Simplified Speech	When the learner develops a level of fluency and can make semantic and grammar generalizations. Also known as the *Advanced Language Proficiency stage*.

Researchers disagree on whether the development of Formulaic Speech and Experimental or Simplified Speech is the same for first language (L1) and second language (L2) learners. Regardless, understanding that a student must go through predictable, sequential stages of language learning helps teachers to recognize the student's progress and respond effectively. Providing comprehensible input will help students advance their language learning at any stage.

Basic Principles of First Language Acquisition

Studies of the basic principles of language learning have concluded that while learning a second language is in many ways similar to learning a first language, there are clear differences.

DIFFERENCES IN LEARNING FIRST AND SECOND LANGUAGES		
LANGUAGE LEARNING PROCESS	**FIRST LANGUAGE (L1)**	**SECOND LANGUAGE (L2)**
Acquisition or Learning Order	All language learners acquire L1 in a more or less universal order.	L2 learners do not go through the same stages as L1 learners. The auxiliary "be" and the copula ("be" used as a main verb) are acquired earlier; the irregular past is acquired later.
Success in Language Learning	All people, unless they suffer from brain damage, learn their language.	This is not necessarily true in L2. Some learners may reach a stage of fossilization.
Objectives	Need to communicate with others and to satisfy physical and psychological needs.	Needs and interests of L2 learners vary with the individual.
Nature of Input	Wide in scope. Received from parents and others around them, media, etc.	Received from different sorts of channels (formal instruction, books, media, etc.).
Cognitive and Affective Factors	These factors are not relevant as language learning is a natural process.	More important than in L1. Same is true of other variables such as age, intelligence, cognitive style, personality, etc.
Time Devoted to LL	No special time required; learning is spontaneous.	Varies considerably according to the individual, number of class hours, opportunities, etc.

The first language of language learners can affect their acquisition of a second language through interference, accent, and code switching.

Interference

According to behaviorist theories, the inability to follow the language patterns of L2 is caused by the negative interference of L1 on L2 when L2 is different from L1. Thus a Spanish speaker may say "To me I likes the dance (i.e., *dancing*)" <A mí me gusta el baile> because of the interference of L1.

Accent

Accent in language learning seems to be more pronounced in older learners than in children. The CRITICAL PERIOD HYPOTHESIS assumes that until a certain age, language occurs naturally. Many theorists argue that language is best learned

> **CRITICAL PERIOD HYPOTHESIS:** assumes that until a certain age, language occurs naturally

before the brain loses its plasticity, which occurs around the age of puberty. Learners who begin their language studies after puberty generally have poorer pronunciation skills and a more pronounced accent.

Code-Switching

CODE-SWITCHING: the mixing of some words, phrases, or idioms from one language with another, perhaps when a word is unknown in the other language

In areas where more than one language is spoken, words from languages other than English enter conversations to facilitate communication. The mixing of Spanish and English is sometimes called "Spanglish." A person who intersperses one language with another is **CODE-SWITCHING**, or mixing some words, phrases, or idioms from one language with another, perhaps when a word is unknown in the other language.

SKILL **Stages of second-language acquisition** *(e.g., silent period, interlanguage,*
4.3 *morpheme acquisition order)*

Interlanguage and Overgeneralization

INTERLANGUAGE: a strategy used by a second-language learner to compensate for his/her lack of proficiency while learning a second language

INTERLANGUAGE is a strategy used by a second-language learner to compensate for his/her lack of proficiency while learning a second language. It cannot be classified as first language (L1), nor can it be classified as a second language (L2), rather it could almost be considered a third language (L3), complete with its own grammar and lexicon. Interlanguage is developed by the learner, in relation to the learner's experiences (both positive and negative) with the second language. Larry Selinker introduced the theory of interlanguage in 1972 and asserted that L2 learners create certain learning strategies, to "compensate" in this in-between period, while the learner acquires the language.

INTERLANGUAGE LEARNING STRATEGIES	
Overgeneralization	Overgeneralization occurs when the learner attempts to apply a rule "across-the-board," without regard to irregular exceptions. For example, a learner is over-generalizing when he/she attempts to apply an /ed/ to create a past tense for an irregular verb, such as *buyed* or *swimmed.*
Simplification	Simplification occurs when the L2 learner uses resources that require limited vocabulary to aid comprehension and allows the learner to listen, read, and speak in the target language at a very elementary level.

Continued on next page

L1 Interference or Language Transfer	L1 Interference or language transfer occurs when a learner's primary language influences his/her progress in the secondary language, L2. Interference most commonly affects pronunciation, grammar structures, vocabulary, and semantics

Selinker theorizes that a psychological structure is "awakened" when a learner begins the process of second language acquisition. He attaches great significance to the notion that the learner and the native speaker would not create similar sounds if they attempted to communicate the same thought, idea, or meaning.

FOSSILIZATION is a term applied by Selinker to the process in which an L1 learner reaches a plateau and accepts that less-than-fluent level, which prevents the learner from achieving L2 fluency. Fossilization occurs when non-L1 forms become fixed in the interlanguage of the L2 learner. L2 learners are highly susceptible to this phenomenon during the early stages.

FOSSILIZATION: a term that describes when an L1 learner reaches a plateau and accepts that less-than-fluent level, which prevents him from achieving L2 fluency

MORPHEME ACQUISITION ORDER IN SECOND LANGUAGE ACQUISITION	
Stage 1	-ing, plural, copula
Stage 2	auxiliary verb, article
Stage 3	irregular past tense verbs
Stage 4	regular past tense verbs, 3rd person singular, possessives

(After Krashen, 1977)

SKILL 4.4 **Types of student motivations** *(intrinsic and extrinsic)* **and their implications for the second-language learning process**

Student Motivation

Researchers Gardner and Lambert (1972) have identified two types of motivation in relation to learning a second language:

- **Instrumental motivation:** Acquiring a second language for a specific reason, such as a job

- **Integrative motivation:** Acquiring a second language to fulfill a wish to communicate within a different culture

Extrinsic (instrumental) motivation is motivation imposed upon the student. He may respond positively or negatively depending on his desire to improve his job requirements, his financial needs, his familial responsibilities, etc. Intrinsic (integrative) motivation is internal motivation—the desire to learn a language for itself or perhaps the desire to know another culture more intimately. One is imposed, the other is longed for.

Neither type stands completely alone. Instructors recognize that motivation can be viewed as either a "trait" or a "state." As a *trait*, motivation is more permanent and culturally acquired, whereas as a *state*, motivation is considered temporary because it fluctuates, depending on rewards and penalties.

SKILL 4.5 Language modeling, comprehensible input, and scaffolding in language learning

Language Modeling

Language teachers are responsible for modeling correct language structures and pronunciation for ELLs. This facilitates the acquisition of new language and enhances the language learning experience for them. Language modeling can also be in the form of examples of work expected from the students.

Comprehensible Input

In language learning, input is defined as the language information or data to which the learner has access. Learners receive input from their parents, their community, TV, the teacher, the textbook, readers, audio and video tapes, other students in the classroom, etc. It is generally accepted that COMPREHENSIBLE INPUT is key to second language learning. Even so, input alone may not lead to second language acquisition. The kind of input must also be taken into consideration.

> **COMPREHENSIBLE INPUT:** the language information or data to which the learner has access

Krashen believes humans acquire language in only one way: by understanding messages—that is, receiving comprehensible input. Krashen defines comprehensible input as i + 1 or input that is just beyond the learner's present ability. In this way, the learner can move from what he knows to the next level in the natural order of acquisition.

> *Krashen defines comprehensible input as i + 1 or input that is just beyond the learner's present ability. In this way, the learner can move from what he knows to the next level in the natural order of acquisition.*

Other theorists report that frequency of certain items in the target language appear to contribute to output (Dulay and Burt, 1974; Schmidt and Frota, 1986). Collier's (1995) research suggests that classes in schools that are highly interactive, emphasizing student problem-solving and discovery through thematic experiences across the curriculum are likely to provide the kind of social setting for natural language acquisition to take place simultaneously with academic and cognitive development. She continues, "Collaborative interaction in which meaning is negotiated with peers is central to the language acquisition process, for both oral and written language development."

Scaffolding

SCAFFOLDING or supporting ELLs consists of demonstrating, guiding, and teaching in a step-by-step process while ELLs are trying to communicate effectively and develop their language skills (Cazden, 1983; Ninio and Bruner, 1976). The amount of scaffolding depends on the support needed and the individual. It allows the ELL to assume more and more responsibility as he or she is able. Once the ELLs feel secure in their abilities, they are ready to move on to the next stage.

Educational scaffolding consists of several linked strategies including: modeling academic language, and contextualizing academic language using visuals, gestures, and demonstrations to help students while they are involved in hands-on learning. Some efficient scaffolding techniques are: providing direction, clarifying purpose, keeping the student on task with proposed rubrics that clarify expectations, offering suggestions for resources, and supplying a lesson or activity without problems.

Tompkins (2006) identified five levels of scaffolding for learning and problem solving to show how ELLs moved from needing considerable support to the independent level where they are ready to solve problems on their own.

Some efficient scaffolding techniques: providing direction, clarifying purpose, keeping the student on task with proposed rubrics that clarify expectations, offering suggestions for resources, and supplying a lesson or activity without problems.

SCAFFOLDING: consists of demonstrating, guiding, and teaching in a step-by-step process while ELLs are trying to communicate effectively and develop their language skills

LEVELS OF SCAFFOLDING FOR LEARNING AND PROBLEM SOLVING	
Modeling	The instructor models orally or through written supports (a paragraph, a paper, an example) the work expected of the ELL. Projects from previous years can provide examples of the type of work expected.
Shared	ELLs use their pooled knowledge of the project (and that of their teacher) to complete the assignment.
Interactive	The teacher allows ELLs to question her on points that need clarification or are not understood, i.e., everyone is a learner. It is especially satisfying for the student when the teacher admits that she does not know the answer and helps the students locate it.
Guided	Well-posed questions, clues, reminders, and examples are all ways of guiding the ELL toward the goal.
Independent	The learner achieves independence and no longer needs educational scaffolding.

COMPETENCY 5
LITERACY

SKILL 5.1 **Relationships between English phonemes and graphemes as well as the differences between English pronunciation and spelling**

PHONEMES: speech sounds

GRAPHEMES: written symbols

Students must learn to identify the approximately 44 sounds of English with their visual counterpart.

The relationship between English **PHONEMES** (speech sound) and **GRAPHEMES** (written symbol) can cause language learners considerable difficulty because English is not a phonetic language as is Spanish, for example. Students must learn to identify the approximately 44 sounds of English with their visual counterpart. Since there are only 26 letters in English, the letters must be combined in different ways to produce the 44 sounds. In elementary schools, much time is devoted to the teaching of phonics. Phonics also tries to convey the spelling rules for the different sounds in English.

Advantages of phonics:

- Students receive the tools for decoding the written word

- Auditory learners can usually associate the sound with the written word

- Emphasis on sound-symbol often transfers to spelling

Disadvantages of phonics:

- Visual learners may not read well with this method

- The rules are not universal

- The numerous exceptions and inconsistencies are problematic for students who process information using logical-mathematical intelligence

(Davis, 2006)

SKILL 5.2 **Conventions of standard written English and the range of genres and rhetorical patterns used in written English**

Standard written English is straightforward and is a reflection of the English character. Most paragraphs begin with a topic sentence followed by supporting details and a conclusion. In longer text, the same structure is followed with the concluding sentence possibly being a transitional sentence leading into the next paragraph. Other cultures have different stylistic forms of writing that reflect their culture, so some students may find it difficult to understand the English text structure.

Text Types that Students Are Exposed To

According to Grellet (1981) students are exposed to

- Novels, short stories, tales, essays, diaries, anecdotes, biographies
- Plays
- Poems, limericks, nursery rhymes
- Letters, postcards, telegrams, notes
- Newspapers and magazines: headlines, articles, editorials, letters to the editor, stop press, classified ads, weather forecast, radio/TV/theater programs
- Specialized articles, reports reviews, essays, business letters, summaries, précis, accounts, pamphlets
- Handbooks, textbooks, guidebooks
- Recipes
- Advertisements, travel brochures, categories
- Puzzles, problems, rules for games
- Instructions, directions, notices, rules and regulations, posters, signs, forms, graffiti, menus, price lists, tickets
- Comic strips, cartoons and caricatures, legends
- Statistics, diagrams, flow/pie charts, time tables, maps
- Telephone directories, dictionaries, phrasebooks

GENRES OF CHILDREN'S LITERATURE		
GENRES	**CHARACTERISTICS**	**TYPES**
Picture Books	Designated as a genre because of format rather than style (Schumm, 2006)	
Traditional Literature	Stories, wise sayings, rhymes passed down by storytellers	Folk tales, fairy tales, cumulative tales, pourqoui tales, noodlehead tales, animal tales, myths, fables, legends, tall tales, rhymes,

Continued on next page

Modern Fantasy	• Similar to traditional literature, but has known author • Characterized by at least one magical element	Modern fairy tales, high fantasy, modern animal tales, science fiction
Contemporary Realistic Fiction	• Main characters are common people, usually about the same age as the audience • Contemporary time frame • Believability • Deals with familiar everyday situations or serious life issues	
Historical Fiction	• Realistic stories set in past (dividing point between past and contemporary varies)	
Multicultural Literature	Works that represent a distinct group through accurate portrayal and rich detail (Hancock, 2000)	
Poetry	Broad category that includes songs and raps, word pictures, novel in form of free verse	Picture-book version of single poem, specialized collections, comprehensive anthologies
Nonfiction	Informational books	Encyclopedias and textbooks, trade books, including real-life adventures and history
Biographies/ Autobiographies	Describes the life or part of the life of a real historical or contemporary individual	Authentic biography, fictionalized biography, collective biography

Rhetorical Patterns Used In English

Rhetorical patterns in academic discourse concern mainly the appeal to reason (persuasion), the appeal to passion or emotion (argumentation), and the appeal to the character and authority of the author (Hyland, 2002).

Academic English usually uses one of the following strategies of development and arrangement of ideas. (There are many exceptions to the following arrangements of ideas.)

STRATEGIES FOR DEVELOPMENT OF ACADEMIC ENGLISH		
STRATEGIES FOR DEVELOPMENT	**PURPOSES**	**ARRANGEMENT OF IDEAS**
Description	Reporting on individual features of a particular subject. • Uses sensory details for support and spatial order	Spatial order
Narration	Studying the changes of a subject over a period of time. Used to: • Tell a story or incident • Explain a process • Explain cause and effect	Chronological order
Classification	Analyzing a subject in relationship to others using one of 3 methods: • Dividing • Defining • Comparing and contrasting	Logical order
Evaluation	Judging the value of a subject. Used to: • Inform people • Persuade them to act or think differently about the topic	Order of importance

SKILL 5.3 Familiarity with current approaches to literacy development

Research into literacy development often centers on whether a top-down or bottom-up strategy is more valid. In a **TOP-DOWN STRATEGY**, emphasis is on the global meaning of a text. In a top down strategy, cues such as the layout of the text (title, length, typeface, and pictures) are studied. Students then make guesses about what is going to happen, and anticipate the contents of the text. In a **BOTTOM-UP STRATEGY**, the reader goes from words and phrases to general understanding.

TOP-DOWN STRATEGY: emphasis is on the global meaning of a text

BOTTOM-UP STRATEGY: the reader goes from words and phrases to general understanding

Grellet (1981) believes that a top-down method is preferred. The reader is more inclined to infer meaning from sentences and paragraphs. In addition, she feels that readers who use a bottom-up strategy may read all texts at the same speed, which is undesirable.

McCarthy (1991) also believes that a top-down strategy is to be preferred, but without neglecting the individual words, phrases, and grammatical devices while striving for meaning.

SKILL 5.4 Stages of English literacy development and the importance of oral language skills to literacy

Characteristics of Reading Stages for ELLs

By building on what the ELL already knows about literacy, language, and experiences in his or her native language, teachers will be able to improve the reading level of the ELL in English.

Children learn to read only once. If they are able to read in their native language, they are able to read in English. It is important for ELLs to increase their vocabulary and knowledge of the structure of English, their second language. By building on what the ELL already knows about literacy, language, and experiences in his or her native language, teachers will be able to improve the reading level of the ELL in English. For this reason, it is necessary to evaluate the ELL in his or her first, native, or heritage language in order to initiate the best reading instruction in English.

Reading stages were first studied by Chall (1983). She proposed six stages of reading that change over time as children progress through school.

1. Pre-reading: Typical of preschool through late kindergarten (also called pre-alphabetic, logographic, pre-conventional)

2. Initial reading or alphabetic decoding: Typical of kindergarten through early second grade (also called alphabetic decoding stage)

3. Confirmation and fluency: Typical of second and third grades

4. Reading to learn: Typical of fourth to eighth grades

5. Multiple points of view: Typical of high school

6. Construction and reconstruction: Typical of college and adulthood

Later studies have modified Chall's work. Newer studies emphasize the integration of processing skills and importance of sound, spelling, and meaning in learning words. These elements develop together on a continuum, so rich text environments are crucial to development of the growth process.

Ehri (1996) developed a continuum of word reading development demonstrating how children master the alphabetic principle:

- The Logographic Phase. Child may:

  - Try to remember words by incidental visual characteristics

  - Treat words as pictograms and make a direct association to meaning

  - Equate the length of the word with its meaning

- The Novice Alphabetic Phase. Child may:

  - Identify first consonant in word; must learn to separate all sounds

  - Rely on letter names to identify word; need to distinguish between letter sounds and their names

  - Confuse similar words; need to decode the whole word, left to right, with sound-symbol links

- The Mature Alphabetic Phase. Child:

  - Can sound out regular, one-syllable words

  - Can increase speed of whole word recognition when decoding becomes accurate

  - Has well-established phonemic awareness

  - Can represent almost every sound with a logical letter choice

  - Can represent and recognize spelling patterns, words of more than one syllable, meaningful parts of words, and basic sight vocabulary

- The Orthographic Phase. Child can:

  - Read words using phonemes, syllabic units, morpheme units, and whole words

  - Use sequential and hierarchical decoding, i.e., notice familiar parts first then can decode unfamiliar parts

  - Remember multisyllabic words

  - Use knowledge of word origin, syntactic role, ending rules, prefix, suffix and root forms to decode words and their meanings

Children cannot retain more than a few dozen sight words, and progress is developed only if they are able to relate letters to sounds. Schumm (2006) emphasizes that not only are the reading level characteristics important, so are the differences between L1 and L2, because these may influence the assumed level of the student. Some of the questions she proposes to elicit these similarities and differences are for further evaluation of reading level characteristics:

Children cannot retain more than a few dozen sight words, and progress is developed only if they are able to relate letters to sounds.

- Is the L1 writing system logographic like Arabic, syllabic like Cherokee, or alphabetic like English and Greek?

- How does the L1 syntax compare with the L2 syntax?

- Are the spelling patterns phonetic with consistent grapheme-phoneme relationships (e.g., Spanish or French) or are there multiple vowel sounds (e.g., English)?

- Do students read from left to right and top to bottom in their L1?

- Are there true cognates (Spanish *instrucción* and English *instruction*) and false cognates (Spanish *librería* <bookstore> and English *library*) that will help or confuse the ELL?

- Are the discourse patterns and writing styles of L1 and L2 similar or different?

- Are questions with known answers asked (teacher questions) or are rhetorical questions asked?

- Is L1 writing style circular, with long sentences and many details (e.g., Spanish) or linear, with the minimum number of facts or supporting details needed to support the main idea (e.g., English)?

> *Research shows that students who are proficient readers in L1 have more reading success in L2.*

> *In general, bilingual education models maintain the idea that ELLs be at least at the level of speech emergence before reading instruction begins. Given the increasing variation of the U.S. school population, however, many believe that it is no longer equitable to wait for oral proficiency before beginning reading instruction.*

Research shows that students who are proficient readers in L1 have more reading success in L2 (Collier and Thomas, 1989: Ovando et al, 2003; and Snow, Burns and Griffin, 1998). This leads us to the question, "What role does the oral second language play in the reading process?" In general, bilingual education models maintain the idea that ELLs be at least at the level of speech emergence before reading instruction begins. Given the increasing variation of the U.S. school population, however, many believe that it is no longer equitable to wait for oral proficiency before beginning reading instruction. Anderson and Roit (1998) argue that reading instruction should be used with certain L2 learners and avoided with others. When instruction is well planned and teachers consider the individual students' needs, all ELLs can benefit from reading instruction in L2.

SKILL 5.5 First-language literacy influences the development of English literacy

Many studies have found that cognitive and academic development in the first language have an extremely important and positive effect on second language schooling (Bialystok, 1991; Collier, 1989, 1992; Garcia, 1994; Genesee, 1987, 1994; Thomas and Collier, 1995). It is important, therefore, that language learners continue to develop their first language skills because the most gifted five-year-old is approximately halfway through the process of first language development. From the ages of 6 to 12, the child continues to acquire subtle phonological distinctions, vocabulary, semantics, syntax, formal discourse patterns, and the complexities of pragmatics in the oral system of their first language (Berko and Gleason, 1993).

These skills can be transferred to acquiring or learning a second language. When ELLs already know how to read and write in their first language, they can transfer many of their primary language skills to their target language. They have already learned the relationship between print and spoken language, that print can be used for many different things, and that writing conveys messages from its author. Grellet (1981) has stated that the "knowledge one brings to the text is often more important than what one finds in it." Thus, teachers can build on this previous knowledge and address specifics in English as they arise.

Collier emphasizes that students who do not reach a threshold of knowledge in their first language, including literacy, may experience cognitive difficulties in their second language (Collier, 1987; Collier and Thomas, 1989, Cummins, 1981, 1991; Thomas and Collier, 1995). Uninterrupted cognitive development is key. It is a disservice to parents and children to encourage the use of second language instead of first language at home, precisely because both are working at a level below their actual cognitive maturity. While non-native speakers in kindergarten through second or third grade may do well if schooled in English part or all of the day, from fourth grade through high school, students with little or no academic or cognitive development in their first language, do less and less well as they move into the upper grades where academic and cognitive demands are greater (Collier, 1995).

> *Many studies have found that cognitive and academic development in the first language have an extremely important and positive effect on second language schooling*

> *When ELLs already know how to read and write in their first language, they can transfer many of their primary language skills to their target language.*

> *While non-native speakers in kindergarten through second or third grade may do well if schooled in English part or all of the day, from fourth grade through high school, students with little or no academic or cognitive development in their first language, do less and less well as they move into the upper grades where academic and cognitive demands are greater (Collier, 1995).*

DOMAIN III
PLANNING, IMPLEMENTING, AND MANAGING INSTRUCTION

PERSONALIZED STUDY PLAN

✗✓ **KNOWN MATERIAL/ SKIP IT**

COMPETENCY 6
INSTRUCTIONAL THEORY

SKILL 6.1 **Characteristics, theoretical foundations, and appropriate use of methods and approaches in second-language learning** *(e.g., the Direct Method, Total Physical Response, the Natural Approach)*

The **DIRECT METHOD** was promoted by Maximilian Berlitz in his language institutes of the same name. The Direct Method uses oral interaction but not translation or L1. The main aim of the courses is to use language as it is used in everyday life. Students learn grammar inductively. Oral communication skills are built up gradually as students became more adept at the new language. Since translation is not used, teachers use mime, sketches, or pantomime in order to convey the meaning of the vocabulary.

For beginning students, **TOTAL PHYSICAL RESPONSE** (Asher, 1982) allows ELLs to participate without forcing speech in the beginning of their introduction to the English language. Using the TPR approach, the instructor issues commands that are carried out by the students. For a slightly different way to achieve the same goals, the popular children's game Simon Says can be a very effective reinforcement of vocabulary items introduced in the classroom.

With the **NATURAL APPROACH** (Krashen and Terrell, 1983), students are introduced to new vocabulary by different experiences. Vividly colored pictures are useful in simulating environments and illustrating concepts. In addition to active involvement with the pictures, learners are able to make choices, answer yes-no questions, and play games.

The **WHOLE LANGUAGE APPROACH** of Goodman, Goodman, and Hood (1989) stresses the importance of developing all four language skills through an integrated approach. In the Language Experience Approach, one of many different instructional strategies used to achieve this goal, children dictate their own story based on a shared experience and then practice reading it until they achieved a firm grasp of the story.

> **DIRECT METHOD:** uses oral interaction but not translation or L1, so student learns grammar inductively and uses L2 as it is used in everyday life

> **TOTAL PHYSICAL RESPONSE:** allows ELLs to participate without forcing speech in the beginning of their introduction to the English language

> **NATURAL APPROACH:** introduces students to new vocabulary through different experiences

WHOLE LANGUAGE APPROACH: stresses the importance of developing all four language skills through an integrated approach

Storytelling is another way of increasing language experiences for ELLs even during very early stages of language acquisition. Wajnryb (1986) claimed that storytelling has many benefits because:

- It is genuine communication
- It is an oral tradition meant to be heard
- It is real
- It is sensual
- It appeals to the affective domain
- It is appreciated by the individual but also creates a sense of community
- It reduces anxiety by forging listening experience
- It is pedagogically positive

By introducing these ESOL techniques, the curriculum is adjusted without isolating the ELLs from mainstream work.

SKILL 6.2 Various instructional delivery models (e.g., push in, pull out, sheltered instruction)

The major models of ESOL programs differ depending on the sources consulted. General consensus recognizes the following program models with different instructional methods used in the different programs.

Immersion Education Models

In immersion education programs, instruction is initiated in the student's non-native language, using the second language as the medium of instruction for both academic content and the second language. Two of these models strive for full bilingualism: one is for language majority students and the other is for language minorities.

Pull-out model

- **English Language Development (ELD)** or **English as a Second Language (ESL):** Pull-out programs include various approaches to teaching English to non-native speakers. In 1997, TESOL standards (Teachers of English to Speakers of Other Languages) defined these approaches as marked by an intent to teach the ELL to communicate in social settings, engage in academic tasks, and use English in socially and culturally appropriate ways. Three well-known approaches to ELD or ESL are:

1. **Grammar-based ESL:** This method teaches about the language, stressing its structure, functions, and vocabulary through rules, drills, and error correction Widdowson (1978) this type of instruction or knowledge of the language refers to as usage.

2. **Communication-based ESL:** This approach emphasizes instruction in English using the language in meaningful contexts. There is little stress on correctness in the early stages and more emphasis on comprehensible input to foster communication and lower anxiety when risk-taking. Widdowson (1978) refers to this type of language knowledge as use.

3. **Content-based ESL:** Instruction in English that attempts to develop language skills and prepare ELLs to study grade-level content material in English. There is emphasis on language, but with graded introduction to content areas, vocabulary, and basic concepts.

- **Structured English immersion:** The goal is English proficiency. ELLs are pulled out for structured instruction in English so that subject matter is comprehensible. Structured English immersion is used with large groups of ELLs who speak the same language and are in the same grade level, or with diverse populations of language minority students. There is little or no L1 language support. Teachers use sheltered instructional techniques and have strong receptive skills in the students' native or heritage language.

- **Submersion with primary language support:** The goal is English proficiency. Bilingual teachers or aides support the minority students who are ELLs in each grade level. In small groups, the ELLs are tutored by reviewing the content areas in their primary language. The teachers use the L1 to support English content classes; ELLs achieve limited literacy in L1.

- **Canadian French immersion (language-majority students):** The goal is bilingualism in French (L2) and English (L1). The targeted population is the language majority. Students are immersed in the L2 for the first 2 years using sheltered language instruction, and then L1 (English) is introduced. The goal is that all students of the majority language (English) become fluent in L2 (French).

- **Indigenous language immersion (endangered languages such as Navajo):** The goal is bilingualism; the program is socially, linguistically, and cognitively attuned to the native culture and community context. This approach supports endangered minority languages and develops academic skills in minority language and culture as well as in the English language and predominant culture.

Push-in model

The push-in model occurs when the ESL teacher goes into the classroom to assist ESL students. ESL teachers need to establish good working relationships and collaborations with the regular teachers in order to co-teach the ELLs. Fulton-Scott and Calvin (1983) suggest that students benefit more from this method because of the interaction with English-proficient speakers.

Sheltered instruction

SHELTERED INSTRUCTION (Specially Designed Academic Instruction in English—SDAIE) is an approach in ESOL teaching that integrates the classroom content with English language instruction. The approach tries to provide mainstream, grade-level content (social studies, math, and science) instruction and promote development of English language proficiency at the same time.

> **SHELTERED INSTRUC-TION:** an approach in ESOL teaching that integrates the classroom content with English language instruction

COMPETENCY 7
TEACHING TECHNIQUES

> **SKILL 7.1** Organizing learning around content and language objectives and aligning learning with standards

> *Much of the instruction ELLs receive should be explicit, with the teacher as a model of expected language- and task-production goals.*

English-language development happens daily. Standards-based instruction is imperative so all ELLs receive instruction that will help them reach their language goals quickly. Language programs organize content into units that incorporate language standards. Much of the instruction ELLs receive should be *explicit*, with the teacher as a model of expected language- and task-production goals. Teachers model and teach the language patterns and vocabulary necessary to allow ELLs to continue their study of language arts and the content (science, math, and social studies) curriculum.

The teacher's obligation is to bring the ELLs up to grade level in academic language as soon as possible using careful planning, excellent teaching methods, and high-quality materials. They are responsible for planning units and creating a learning environment conducive to English Language Development (ELD). They must also provide the ELL with constructive feedback about the accuracy of oral and written work.

STUDENT-CENTERED LEARNING focuses on the needs of the student while taking into account his/her abilities, interests, and learning styles. The teacher takes on the role of a facilitator, and the students assume active roles and the responsibility for their own learning. In student-centered learning, or active learning, the teacher must plan global goals and help the students achieve them. For example, in a science unit on ecology and the environment, students want to study recycling. It is up to the teacher to incorporate the science unit's objectives and standards in the process, and, with the students' help, establish rubrics for evaluation. Using these techniques, ELLs are able to achieve success in both the English language and grade-level content.

> **STUDENT-CENTERED LEARNING:** focuses on the needs of the student while taking into account his/her abilities, interests, and learning styles

SKILL 7.2 Language instruction should be age appropriate

Language instruction should be age appropriate. Most activities that teachers use in the classroom can easily be adapted to provide age-appropriate activities. For children, instruction should include games and game-like activities. As ELLs age, games are still appropriate, but most students expect a more academic environment where their questions about grammar (and other language related topics), answered in a serious vein. Even so, teachers should use fun activities to lighten up heavy lessons and keep motivation high. When using lighter activities, teachers may want to explain their reasons for particular activities to teens and adults, because they often will question the value of such activities in language learning.

SKILL 7.3 Collaboration with general education and content area teachers

No single research-based teaching model has been shown to be more effective than another. The following examples show several models that are currently in use in the classroom (Friend and Bursuck, 2005).

- **One teach, one observe:** One teacher teaches the entire group while one observes and collects data on an individual student, a small group of students, or the entire class.

- **One teach, one assist:** One teacher instructs the entire group of students while the other professional is circulating among the students providing assistance.

- **Parallel teaching:** Two professionals split the group of students in half and simultaneously provide the same instruction.

- **Station teaching:** The teachers divide instruction into two, three, or even more nonsequential components, and each is addressed in a separate area of the room, with each student participating at each station.

- **Alternative teaching:** A teacher takes a small group of students to the side of the room for instruction.

- **Team teaching:** Professionals who have built a strong collaborative relationship and have complementary teaching styles fluidly share the instructional responsibilities of the entire student group.

Other teaching models include:

- **Peer tutoring:** Peers are used to tutor students who are weak in certain skills. This approach benefits both students—the tutor reinforces his/her learning, and the tutored gains valuable insights into learning.

- **Educational technologies:** Technology has two advantages over humans in tutoring students: Students can practice the skills they need in a nonjudgmental environment, and the machine never becomes tired.

| SKILL 7.4 | Various methods for promoting students' acquisition of productive and receptive language |

Listening Comprehension

The teacher must use every possible strategy to make stories and information comprehensible and to make both verbal and nonverbal responses available as a means of demonstrating comprehension. Repetition, gestures, facial expressions, realia, illustrations, slowing the pacing to allow students time to make connections, and tone of voice—all are tools the teacher can use to increase comprehension.

Repetition, gestures, facial expressions, realia, illustrations, slowing the pacing to allow students time to make connections, and tone of voice—all are tools the teacher can use to increase comprehension.

Acceptable responses can vary from the simplest nonverbal response ("Point to the volcano." "Draw a volcano.") to yes/no responses ("Is this the volcano?") to those requiring the expression of the new vocabulary ("What do we call this kind of mountain?") to the sorts of complex assessments that would be required of ELA students ("Using the Internet for research, make a list of currently active volcanoes").

Students can be shown how to scan unfamiliar material for specific words or phrases, ("What was the first thing Elena said?"), to listen for tone ("Does Jack like the giant? How do you know?") and to watch for discourse markers ("Once upon a time," "after a while," "until he got home," "in the end").

Speaking

The teacher must provide multiple opportunities for oral communication. These might include individual teacher conferences, in which the student speaks one-on-one with the teacher; group activities such as brainstorming and problem solving, expressing an opinion in a group discussion, and role-playing and reenactments; and individual presentations such as recitations, summarizing or retelling stories, and starting conversations with questions. For example, students can practice varying speech according to different purposes, audiences, and subject matter by "translating" a message as it would be delivered to a teacher, a parent, or a friend.

Reading

A variety of strategies to increase fluency, such as the following, may help the ELL with learning to read fluently:

- Duet reading, when the student reads aloud together with the teacher, helps the student develop proper intonation and pacing.

- Listen/repeat exercises, including short dialogs between teacher and student or between two students.

- Choral reading, when the entire class reads aloud together, starting and stopping and emphasizing at the same points.

- Singing, which is difficult to forget. Simple common expressions set to familiar tunes, such as "Happy Birthday" or "Are You Sleeping?" can be quickly invented and help develop fluency.

Second-language acquisition is a jigsaw process, in which a student acquires comprehension of a word, a phrase, or a concept in ways that may seem random and unmanageable. The imposition of systematic vocabulary development, whether content-related or grouped by phonics or grammatical structures, relieves anxiety and lowers the affective filter.

> *Second-language acquisition is a jigsaw process, in which a student acquires comprehension of a word, a phrase, or a concept in ways that may seem random and unmanageable.*

- Armed with recognizable text connectors (*and, but, because, until, unless,* etc.), a student can more easily break down text into manageable segments.

- Use of the dictionary, with its many abbreviations and pronunciation symbols, empowers the student to research new words with confidence.

- Recognizing common morphemes such as the prefix *un-* can help students decode *un*-familiar and *un*-known words (without becoming *un*-happy).

A variety of scaffolding techniques to help students recognize features of different types of texts is useful in developing independent readers. For instance:

- Students can be taught key words to help differentiate fact from opinion ("I believe"; "it seems to me…").

- Students can draw arrows between listed events in the text to determine what is a cause and what is an effect.

- Students can be taught to make inferences ("The old woman was crying. What does that tell us?").

- Students can make text-to-self connections ("Have you ever…?").

- Students can evaluate credibility ("Is the wolf a reliable narrator? Why or why not?").

Writing

According to the research of Dr. Jill Kerper Mora of San Diego State University, ELD student writing can be expected to lag behind oral language development by one or two levels. The natural progression goes from words to sentences to paragraphs to narratives (Mora, 1993).

An example of an effective strategy for addressing the disparity between oral and written language development is the use of dictations. The ELL dictates as the teacher writes the story or information the learner presents. This helps solidify the correspondence between oral and written language and makes it clear that writing is another way to express the same thoughts that are spoken.

Spelling often reflects sound-symbol correspondence, and the syntactical errors present in speech also occur in writing. Evaluation can be done in many ways: teacher modeling, peer modeling, and direct error correction. The English Learner's editing skills will develop along with the ability to compare his/her own work with models. ELLs will learn that their writing needs to be modified in order to be understood by others and learn how to reorder text elements to clarify meaning.

Penmanship is one area that has been left behind in the rush to firm up language and math instruction for ELD students. But penmanship is a legitimate part of language instruction because the development of handwriting contributes to the development of other language processes: directionality, graphophonics, and spelling. Students who write with ease are less impeded in their efforts to communicate and more willing to put effort into written communication.

The teacher knows that the student gradually develops a sense of purpose for writing and understands the difference between writing with explanation, entertainment, or persuasion as its purpose. The student will also be able to use

Penmanship is a legitimate part of language instruction because the development of handwriting contributes to the development of other language processes: directionality, graphophonics, and spelling.

information gained in research in personal writing and within the context of his or her own purpose as writing skills develop.

Direct instruction in grammar and spelling has had disappointing effects on students' writing. Teachers have not achieved much success with extensive error correction, either. The most successful teaching of language conventions has been the presentation of well-written materials. A good reader becomes a good writer as the self-editing process develops and good models are available. A teacher is most likely to be successful if he/she keeps a variety of well-written and easily understood examples of both written and spoken English available to the students.

> *The most successful teaching of language conventions has been the presentation of well-written materials. A good reader becomes a good writer as the self-editing process develops and good models are available.*

SKILL 7.5 Strategies for teaching language skills both discretely and integratively

For ELLs who are not literate in their first language, or are literate in their first language but are below grade level in their second language, remedial instruction may be necessary to bring them up to grade level.

For the student who is not literate, the same steps used for native speakers will have to be followed, though perhaps at a slightly more accelerated pace, depending on the age of the student learning these discrete skills.

Peregoy and Boyle (2008) state that the following sequence of phonics instruction usually recommended for native speakers would probably be helpful to non-native speakers as well:

- Single consonants at the beginning of words

- Short and long vowels

- Letter patterns and word families (onsets and rimes)

- Digraphs (e.g., *th*, *ch*, *ph*) and blends (e.g., *cl*, *bl*, *tr*, *cr*, *pr*)

Remember: Phonics is a means to an end (comprehension), not isolated rules to be memorized.

> *Remember: Phonics is a means to an end (comprehension), not isolated rules to be memorized.*

The student who is literate in a native language with an alphabet similar to English (e.g., Spanish, German, or French) is likely to need less work in phonics because the consonants are similar. English vowels and their spellings cause difficulties for most readers, including native speakers, so extra care should be given to instruction in this area. Reading aloud, journal writing, games with sound/symbol correspondence, and different kinds of computer software for beginning readers can help the student get extra practice in this area.

> *English vowels and their spellings cause difficulties for most readers, including native speakers, so extra care should be given to instruction in this area.*

Integrated skills can be practiced following the same methods used to teach language arts to children who are literate in the English language, but making the adaptations needed based upon the native language of the ELL. Some children may have to learn a new alphabet; others may have to learn to read in a different direction (for example, from left to right versus from right to left), and others may have problems with the "hero" concept of Western literature.

Other considerations include:

- The curriculum should be learner-centered and designed for meaningful learning.

- Each lesson or unit should be based on a theme.

- Reading and writing are reinforced as competency-building tools.

- Language skills are assessed with the learners applying new skills and competencies to solve new problems.

- Varying cultural experiences and themes are included in the curriculum.

Adapted from: the Florida Department of Education's Language Arts Through ESOL: A Guide for ESOL Teachers and Administrators (1999).

SKILL 7.6 Strategies for supporting content-based language learning

The cognitive skills of being able to think clearly, understand key concepts, and express oneself are skills that generally transfer from one content area to another.

Content-based ELD is more than having knowledge. It represents skills that are needed to acquire knowledge of content and make it easier for the student to read and write in the discipline (Diaz-Rico, 2008). The cognitive skills of being able to think clearly, understand key concepts, and express oneself are skills that generally transfer from one content area to another. For content-based instruction to be effective, students, content teachers, and language teachers must work together to achieve the state standards in the content area while developing the English language skills needed by the ELLs. Planning systematic instruction that covers vocabulary, concepts, and structures is vital to content mastery (Snow, 1993).

Planning systematic instruction that covers vocabulary, concepts, and structures is vital to content mastery.

Strategies to implement content-based learning include, but are not limited to, the following:

- Access ELLs' prior knowledge

- Contextualize a lesson's key concepts and language

- Modify and augment state-mandated, content-area textbooks

- Demonstrate or model learning tasks

- Use questions to promote critical-thinking skills

- Provide ELLs with explicit instruction in metacognitive and cognitive strategies

- Develop ELLs' academic vocabulary

- Provide ELLs with opportunities to learn and use academic vocabulary

- Provide ELLs with opportunities to use English for communicative purposes

- Assess lesson content through various means

- Provide comprehensible and meaningful feedback

SKILL 7.7 Lessons and activities that help students become more effective language learners by developing their cognitive and metacognitive strategies

Metacognitive Strategies

The ESOL teacher is responsible for helping students become aware of their own individual learning strategies and constantly improve and add to those strategies. Each student should have his/her own toolbox of skills for planning, managing, and evaluating the language-learning process.

Metacognitive strategies for ELL students include:

- **Centering your learning:** Review a key concept or principle and link it to prior knowledge; make a firm decision to pay attention to the general concept; ignore input that is distracting; and learn skills in the proper order.

- **Arranging and planning your learning:** The following strategies help the learner maximize the learning experience: Take the time to understand how a language is learned; create optimal learning conditions, i.e., regulate noise, lighting, and temperature; obtain the appropriate books and materials; and set reasonable long-term and short-term goals.

- **Evaluate your learning:** The following strategies help learners assess their learning achievements: Keep track of errors that prevent further progress and keep track of progress, e.g., reading more quickly now than in the previous month.

> The ESOL teacher is responsible for helping students become aware of their own individual learning strategies and constantly improve and add to those strategies.

Cognitive Strategies

Cognitive strategies are vital to second-language acquisition; their most salient feature is the manipulation of the second language. The most basic strategies are: practicing, receiving and sending messages; analyzing and reasoning; and creating structure for input and output, which can be remembered by the acronym PRAC.

> The most basic cognitive strategies are: practicing, receiving and sending messages; analyzing and reasoning; and creating structure for input and output, which can be remembered by the acronym PRAC.

- Practicing: These strategies promote the learner's grasp of the language. Practice constant repetition, make attempts to imitate a native speaker's accent, concentrate on sounds, and practice in a realistic setting.

- Receiving and sending messages: These strategies help the learner quickly locate salient points and then interpret meaning. Skim through information to determine "need to know" vs. "nice to know"; and use available resources (print and nonprint) to interpret messages.

- Analyzing and reasoning: Use general rules to understand the meaning, then work into specifics; and break down unfamiliar expressions into parts.

- Creating structure for input and output: Choose a format for taking meaningful notes, practice summarizing long passages, and use highlighters as a way to focus on main ideas or important specific details.

SKILL 7.8 Techniques that help students activate prior knowledge and support appropriate transfer of language and literacy skills from L1 to L2

Prior Knowledge

> SCHEMA: the framework around information that is stored in the brain

A SCHEMA is the framework around information that is stored in the brain. As new information is received, schemata are activated to store the new information. By connecting what is known with what is being learned, understanding is achieved and learning can take place. Schemata, then, refer to the prior knowledge students have when beginning a new language and are a valuable asset that needs to be exploited in their language learning. The schema theory (Carrell and Eisterhold, 1983) is used to explain how the brain processes knowledge and how these representations facilitate comprehension and learning. If students lack sufficient prior knowledge, they cannot be expected to understand the new lesson.

Children may have prior educational experiences on which to build their new language and literacy skills, or they may not. However, even children who have no or little formal education may have been taught the alphabet or simple mathematics by their parents. Children from oral cultures may have quite sophisticated language structures already in place on which to base new language learning.

Positive and Negative Language Transfer

L1 TRANSFER refers to the effect the native tongue has on the language being acquired. It can be positive or negative. Examples of negative transfer are illustrated in many of the errors ELLs make when using the new language; for instance, when some Chinese learners overuse expressions of regret when apologizing because in their native language it is customary to so.

Positive transfer occurs when similar structures in the L1 facilitate the learning of the new language. An example would be when cognates are able to transfer to the target language.

> **L1 TRANSFER:** the effect the native tongue has on the language being acquired

Activating Prior Knowledge

Teachers activate prior knowledge by:

- Introducing vocabulary before content

- Asking questions about a topic

- Asking questions about topics related to the new information

- Brainstorming about the new topic

- Using graphic organizers such as K (what we know), W (what we want to know), L (what we learned) charts

> **SKILL 7.9** **Activities and assignments that provide students with authentic language use and meaningful interaction in English**

Communication must be meaningful and purposeful for students to learn. If students see no purpose in the exercises, they may not even try. Teachers can have students engage in real-life activities, both written and oral, to develop communication skills.

> *Communication must be meaningful and purposeful for students to learn.*

Zainuddin (2007) lists the key features of communicative language teaching as described by Nunan (1991):

- Focuses on meaning through interaction in the target language

- Uses materials or texts that reflect authentic or real-world language

- Allows learners to rehearse language used outside the classroom by focusing on language forms or skills and the learning process

- Focuses on previous knowledge, experiences, or skills learners bring into the classroom as important contributors to language learning

- Plans a careful link between classroom language and real-world language

> *Communication is paramount, even if it contains errors or misstatements. Students need to interact with the teacher and their peers to advance their communication skills.*

Communication is paramount, even if it contains errors or misstatements. Students need to interact with the teacher and their peers to advance their communication skills.

Some possibilities for oral work are:

- Work on dialogs and create their own

- Hold mock telephone conversations

- Conduct surveys with other classmates or teachers

- Fill-in-the-gap exercises by talking with other classmates

- Give me a word that (dances/runs/is blue/is cold)… (In this exercise, students call out answers to teacher's question.)

For writing, some possibilities are (Zainuddin, 2007):

- Use labels and captions to explain bulletin board pictures or other displays

- Use order forms for purchasing classroom supplies for classroom activities

- Write checks to pay for classroom book orders

- Write personal letters to share news with a friend

- Write scripts for role plays or acting out stories

- Write essays using different forms, e.g.:

    – Enumeration: To list information in steps or chronologically

    – Comparison/contrast: To show how things differ or are the same

    – Problem/solution: To present a problem and a possible solution

    – Cause/effect: To show a relationship

    – Thesis/proof: To present an idea and persuade others of its validity

---

SKILL 7.10 Best practices for teaching English literacy to both literate and nonliterate English-language learners

The teacher needs to have a variety of ways to model and provide opportunities for guided and independent practice to achieve language and content objectives.

As an example, teaching the numbers from one to ten to a pre-beginning class could be done in the following way:

- Show the numerals and pronounce the words. Have students repeat the pronunciation.

- Say the numerals in mixed-up order and ask students to hold up the correct number of fingers.

- Dictate the numerals in mixed-up order and ask students to write the numerals they hear.

- Ask selected students to tell the teacher their phone numbers (or a made-up phone number if they don't want to reveal the real one), and write the number on the board as it is spoken.

- Using the telephone directory, students dictate five or ten real telephone numbers to each other, working with a partner. The partner watches and corrects what the other student writes.

- After practicing the question, "What's your phone number?", the students ask as many classmates as possible and write their responses.

- The teacher then asks the class, "What is Carolina's phone number?", and someone who is not Carolina responds while the rest of the students verify the response.

COMPETENCY 8
MATERIALS

SKILL 8.1 **Locating, selecting, modifying, and/or creating instructional materials that support individual students' learning styles and needs**

Teachers are masters of locating, selecting, modifying and/or creating instructional materials that support their students' needs. To do this, they analyze their student's individual needs and adapt materials for them. On the classroom level, this usually means adapting state- or district-issued materials and making them comprehensible to their ELLs.

By introducing these ESOL techniques, the curriculum is adjusted without isolating the ELLs from mainstream work.

See also Skill 6.1

SKILL 8.2 Selecting culturally responsive, age-appropriate, and linguistically accessible teaching materials and resources

Language-rich environments are crucial when dealing with ELLs in the classroom. No two people learn alike, so diverse materials on the same subject may help the student bridge the gap between prior knowledge and knowledge to be acquired.

Students with little or no English or previous educational experience may be taught in their native language when possible. Research shows that, contrary to previous beliefs, students who are taught content in their native or heritage language are able to receive simultaneous language instruction in English to their benefit (Slavin and Cheung, 2003).

For those students who have reached a certain level of competency in English, scaffolding is recommended. ELL students need extra help with vocabulary, linguistic complexities, idioms, prefixes and suffixes, and false cognates. (Teachers who are able can easily increase ELLs' vocabulary using cognate instruction.)

For further suggestions, see Skill 16.1.

Note: The resources in this skill are concerned not only with learning, but in many cases also deal with the socio-linguistic areas of culture.

SKILL 8.3 Resources *(e.g., audiovisual aids, realia, computer software)* **that support ESL and content instruction**

Most ESL school programs come with appropriate audiovisual support and are available to individual teachers at the school or district level. Computer software from different sources, is also available in most schools and numerous programs can be downloaded for free from Internet sources.

Realia is often obtainable from the students themselves (when teaching about different cultures). For scientific and mathematical realia, materials can be purchased from school supply houses.

Atkinson and Hansen (1966-1967) published the first study of the use of computers in reading instruction. Students at Stanford University accessed reading lessons similar to traditional worksheets on a mainframe computer. Now, the computer is used in all aspects of our lives, and today's students are often assigned laptop computers by their school district to use as a critical part of their learning experience. As technology continues to grow and change, more textbooks are available in digital form.

Blanton and Menendez (2006 in Schumm, ed., *Reading Assessment and Instruction for All Learners*) mention seven categories in which computers are used in reading instruction:

- Game applications, such as Reader Rabbit, Missing Link, and Reading Blaster
- General applications, such as Microsoft Word, PowerPoint, Hyperstudio, Kid Pix, and Story Book Weaver
- Access applications, such as Google and Netscape
- Tutoring applications, such as Watch Me Read
- Thinking and problem-solving applications, such as Oregon Trail, SimCity, SimEarth, and Zoombinis Island Odyssey
- Communication applications, such as e-mail and online discussion spaces
- Integrated learning systems (ILSs), such as the Waterford Early Reading Program, Fast ForWord, and Read 180

COMPETENCY 9
MANAGING THE CLASSROOM AND STUDENTS

Student performance may be affected by various factors *(e.g., age, limited formal schooling, educational interruptions)*

Age

According to Ellis (1985), age does not affect the route (order) of second language acquisition (SLA). Thus, children and adults acquire language in the same order; that is, they go through the same stages. With respect to rate of acquisition, teens appear to surpass both children and adults, especially in learning the grammatical

Children and adults acquire language in the same order; that is, they go through the same stages.

system (Snow and Hoefnagel-Hohle, 1978). Older learners seem to be more efficient learners. The achievement of a foreign language is strongly related to the amount of time spent on the language, and the earlier a second language is started, the better the pronunciation (Burstall et al., 1974). Krashen (1982) disagrees, believing instead that SLA is related to the amount of comprehensible input (i.e., the younger child will receive more comprehensible input) and that younger learners are more open emotionally to SLA.

Other theorists have formulated different hypotheses about age in SLA related to affective factors. In the Critical Period Hypothesis, Penfield and Roberts (1959) state that the first ten years are the best age for SLA because the brain retains its plasticity. After puberty, this plasticity disappears and the flexibility required for SLA is lost. Guiora et al. (1972) believe that around the age of puberty, the ability to acquire native-like pronunciation of the foreign language is no longer present.

Cognitive explanations are also used to explain the effects of age on SLA. These theories state that children are more prone to use their Language Acquisition Device (LAD), while adults are better able to use their inductive reasoning because of more fully developed cognitive faculties. Rosansky (1975) explains SLA in terms of Piaget's "period of concrete operations." Rosansky believes the child is more open and flexible to new language than an adult, who identifies more closely with the differences between the native language and the language to be acquired. Krashen (1982) believes that adolescents and adults probably have greater access to comprehensible input than children and that this rather than age itself, is the real causative variable.

Level of L1 Language Proficiency

Children who are just beginning their education may be able to stay in the general classroom for instruction while older children may need to have specific language items (such as phonemes, syntax, pragmatics, and lexis) taught in specialized classes that take advantage of L1 while teaching the content areas. Nevertheless, McLaughlin (1990) states that the more proficient a learner is in L1, the more the learner understands about language structures and the better he or she is able to use that knowledge to help make language choices when communicating in L2.

> In the Critical Period Hypothesis, Penfield and Roberts (1959) state that the first ten years are the best age for SLA as the brain retains its plasticity. After puberty, this plasticity disappears and the flexibility required for SLA is lost.

> The more proficient a learner is in L1, the more the learner understands about language structures and the better he or she is able to use that knowledge to help make language choices when communicating in L2.

Level of L1 Literacy

Cummins' (1981) Interdependence Hypothesis claims that the degree of knowledge and skill evident in L1 will determine the ease of transfer to L2. Thus, it will take a student who has L1 proficiency but is only an emergent reader in L1 longer to achieve proficiency in L2 than a student who is orally proficient in his or her L1 and in L1 reading ability.

Personality

It isn't clear from research whether or not extroversion or introversion affects second language learning. It has been assumed that extroversion leads to better L2 acquisition, but confusing definitions of different competencies make this unclear. However, it is generally assumed that extroverted students are chattier and develop more communicative competence. Entwhistle and Entwhistle (1970) found that introverted students developed better study habits and had high overall language proficiency.

Despite inconclusive evidence, tolerance of ambiguity is considered another trait of a good language learner. Budner (1964) developed a scale to define the language learner as either one who is comfortable in novel, complex, or insoluble situations (tolerance of ambiguity), or one who perceives these situations as a threat (intolerance of ambiguity). Naiman et al. (1978), using Budner's scale, claim that tolerance of ambiguity correlates to listening comprehension scores but not to imitation test scores.

> Budner (1964) developed a scale to define the language learner as one who is comfortable in novel, complex, or insoluble situations (tolerance of ambiguity), or one who perceives these situations as a threat (intolerance of ambiguity).

Another personality trait that affects language learning is anxiety. MacIntyre and Gardner (1987) believe that anxiety affects the three main stages involved in language learning: input, processing, and output. Scovel (1978) studied the distinction between facilitating and debilitating anxiety. Facilitating anxiety helps the learner because the learner wants to do well and succeed, while debilitating anxiety limits or holds the learner back from performing well because he cannot help himself.

The effects of risk-taking and inhibition also have conflicting evidence with regard to their effect on language learning. McClelland et al. (1953) found that risk-taking is necessary to rapid progress in L2. Krashen (1981) maintains that the affective filter develops as adolescents reach puberty; therefore, they become more self-conscious and less willing to take risks than younger children. Other studies show similar results. Still, the instructor needs to be aware that most of this research was done in psychological laboratories and involves out-of-context behavior with tasks of no practical significance for language learners. Consequently, this research may be of questionable validity.

While an ELL's personality traits are probably unchangeable, the teacher can still encourage certain attitudes towards language learning that could possibly have a positive effect on the ELL's personality profile.

- Respect for the target language (TL), TL speakers, and TL culture

- Emphasis on the practical and positive aspects of language learning

- Confidence in the teacher

Preferred Learning Styles and Modalities

A student's **LEARNING STYLE** includes cognitive, affective, and psychological behaviors that indicate the learner's characteristic and consistent way of perceiving, interacting with, and responding to the learning environment (Willing, 1988).

Willing (1988) identified four main learning styles used by ESL learners in Australia:

- Concrete learning style: People-oriented, emotional, and spontaneous

- Analytic learning style: Object-orientated, with a capacity for making connections and inferences

- Communicative learning style: Autonomous, prefers social learning, likes making decisions

- Authority-orientated learning style: Defers to the teacher, does not enjoy learning by discovery, intolerant of facts that do not fit (ambiguity)

Reid (1987) identified four perceptual learning tendencies:

- Visual learning: Learning mainly from seeing words in books, on the board, etc.

- Auditory learning: Learning by hearing words spoken, from oral explanations, and from listening to tapes or lectures

- Kinesthetic learning: Learning by experience, by being involved physically in classroom experiences

- Tactile learning: Hands-on learning, learning by doing, working on models, lab experiments, etc.

> **LEARNING STYLE:**
> includes cognitive, affective, and psychological behaviors that indicate the learner's characteristic and consistent way of perceiving, interacting with, and responding to the learning environment

Educational Experience

ELLs come to the United States for many different reasons: a better life, fleeing war zones, oppressive governments, or economic difficulties. In many cases, ELLs have entered the school system in their native land and done very well. In other cases, the ELLs have had little or no educational experience. In both cases, it is imperative that previous to or upon enrollment, assessment of the student takes place—if possible in their L1. By building on their previous knowledge with regard to literacy, language, and experience, L2 instruction will be more successful (Au, 1993, 2002; Ovando et al., 2006).

Shumm (2006) lists questions to discover similarities and differences between L1 and L2 that may be useful for further evaluation of reading level characteristics.

See also Skill 5.4

It is imperative that previous to or upon enrollment, assessment of the student take place—if possible in their L1.

Disabilities

Students with disabilities are guaranteed an education under Public Law 94-142 of 1975. A key feature of the law is the requirement for an individualized educational program (IEP) for any student receiving special funds for special education. This said, the classification of many ELLs or the "dumping" of ELLs in special education classes has been of concern to many educators. Those testing ELLs for placement in different classes must be certain that the tests used are both reliable and valid. Reliability can be established using multiple assessment measures, objective tests, multiple raters, and clearly specified scoring criteria (Valdez-Pierce, 2003). For a test to be valid, it must first be reliable (Goh, 2004).

LEARNING DISABILITIES are physical, emotional, cognitive, or social components that severely limit what is considered to be "normal" functioning behavior. Children who fall into this category can be one or more of the following: emotionally challenged, hearing, vision or speech impaired, and/or learning disabled.

LEARNING DISABILITIES: physical, emotional, cognitive, or social components that severely limit what is considered to be "normal" functioning behavior

SIMILARITIES BETWEEN SECOND LANGUAGE DEVELOPMENT AND LEARNING DISABILITIES	
Educators have numerous assessment tools to evaluate the proficiency level of an L2 learner. They also have various assessment tools to determine if an L1 learner has a disability, whether physical, emotional, or learning. However, assessment tools to determine whether an L2 learner has a learning disability are not currently available. The most reliable method to date is observation and interpretation.	The typical blueprint that L2 learners seem to follow in terms of developing their pronunciation skills can be easily confused with a learning disability, because both groups of learners have difficulties in the following areas: omission, substitution, distortion, and addition (Lue, 2001). And, of course, there are some L2 learners with learning disabilities. The following are examples of the problem areas: • Omission: The L1/L2 learner omits a phoneme (the smallest unit of a word). For example: the L1/L2 learner pronounces _ar instead of *bar*. • Substitution: The L1/L2 learner substitutes a phoneme. For example: the L1/L2 learner pronounces *take* instead of *rake*. • Distortion: The L1/L2 learner pronounces a phoneme incorrectly, and the sound produced is not considered normal. For example: the L1/L2 learner pronounces the phoneme *three* as *free*. • Addition: The L1/L2 learner adds an additional syllable to a word. For example, a learner pronounces the word *liked* as *like-id*.

SKILL 9.2 Classroom management and the learning environment for English-language learners

Effective classroom management begins with preplanning and planning. By planning each day's lesson and gathering or preparing all the materials needed for the class, the teacher will be an effective manager and gain student's respect. By preplanning each lesson, the teacher anticipates student questions, information needed, and the appropriate directions to carry out tasks successfully.

During the first days of the course or year, the teacher should discuss his or her inflexible rules (such as "No making fun of others' pronunciation or grammar—we are all here to learn") and invite students to help him or her establish other rules needed for good classroom functioning. Rules should be kept to a minimum.

Students want structure and need limits even though they will test both. They also expect teachers to treat them with dignity and be consistent and fair in enforcing classroom rules.

Students want structure and need limits even though they will test both. They also expect teachers to treat them with dignity and be consistent and fair in enforcing classroom rules. They will quickly let a teacher know if they believe that partiality has been shown to other students.

Teachers need to anticipate disruptive situations or inappropriate behaviors before they happen. Eye contact; moving around the room; short, quiet comments to the disruptive student; and talking privately with students who misbehave avoid power struggles and face-saving acting-out. Stronger measures, especially those that threaten the safety or orderliness of the classroom, require immediate referral to the appropriate administrator along with a discipline referral form.

Effective classroom management not only encompasses behavior, it also covers the working atmosphere of the classroom. Cooperative group work is based on the premise that many cultures are more comfortable working in collaborative groups. While this is true, however, many students may feel that the teacher is the only academic authority in the classroom and, as such, should be the only one in class. Different students feel more comfortable with different instructional formats than others. This may be due to both cultural and individual preferences. By balancing group work with teacher-directed instruction, both points of view can be accommodated.

Care should be taken in using ability grouping. An *Imperiled Generation* (1988), by the Carnegie Foundation, reported on the harmful effects of ability grouping. Ability grouping:

- Carries a social stigma

- Promotes negative feelings about school in low achievers

- Hinders academic progress for average and low achievers

- Often widens the gap between high and low achieving students

Slavin's research (2003) shows that both low achievers and high achievers can benefit from mixed-ability cooperative learning groups that hold individuals accountable for achieving group goals. Low achievers are more challenged, improve their self-image, and are more willing to learn.

Key features to group learning projects are:

- Arranging the classroom furniture to ensure group interaction

- Assigning students to groups to ensure a mixture of gender, ethnicity, linguistic level, and academic levels

- Meaningful tasks

- Stating objectives as group objectives and clarifying expectations precisely

- Assigning each student a role or job

- Monitoring group work during the task

- Assessing both the individual and group achievements

> *Eye contact; moving around the room; short, quiet comments to the disruptive student; and talking privately with students who misbehave avoid power struggles and face-saving acting-out.*

SKILL 9.3 Using correction and constructive feedback and their implications for student learning and motivation

Ur (1996) defines feedback as "information given to the learner about his or her performance of a learning task, usually with the objective of improving this performance." This can be as simple as a thumbs-up, a grade of 75% on a quiz or test, a raised eyebrow when the student makes a mistake, or comments in the margin of an essay.

Feedback has two main aspects: assessment and correction.

Feedback has two main aspects: assessment and correction. Typically, a grade assigned on a written paper, saying "No" to an oral response, simply calling on another student, or a comment such as "Fair" at the end of a written paragraph are used in the language classroom as ways of assessing performance. In correction, comments on a specific aspect of the ELL's performance are given: The teacher may suggest better or additional alternatives, give an explanation of why the ELL's answer is incorrect or partially correct, or elicit a better response from the student.

Research suggests that not all errors need correcting.

Research suggests that not all errors need correcting. Different theories look at mistakes in different ways:

- **Audio-lingualism:** Learners should make few mistakes because they learn in small, controlled steps, so corrections are meaningless.

- **Interlanguage:** Mistakes are an important factor in language learning; by correcting them the learner's interlanguage approaches the target language (Selinker, 1972, 1992).

- **Communicative approach:** Not all mistakes need to be corrected. Correct only those mistakes that interfere with meaning.

- **Monitor theory:** Correction does not lead to language acquisition. Learners need comprehensible input so that they can acquire the target language (Krashen, 1982).

SKILL 9.4 Providing students with a language-, text-, and print-rich environment at an appropriate level

Learning to read in English is one of the most important skills an ELL can achieve. For students already familiar with the concept of reading, the process may be relatively painless, but for those unfamiliar with the concept of reading, it is long and arduous. Teachers must make every effort to create an age-appropriate, language-, text-, and print-rich environment in order to emphasize the importance of reading.

Diaz-Rico (2008) suggests the following items to create such an environment:

- Bulletin boards with words and pictures
- Aquariums and terrariums labeled with the names of their inhabitants
- Calendars with children's birthdays
- Displays of students' stories and booklets
- Student-run post office
- Library corner with book displays
- Labels on objects in several languages
- Magnet letters, printing sets, typewriters, and computers available
- Picture dictionaries, both commercial and student-made
- Listening centers with audio-taped books for read-along
- Order blanks, shopping lists, and notepads at play centers
- Menus available from restaurants
- Advertising flyers to cut and paste
- Weekly words collected on hanger mobiles
- Bulletin boards with week's learning
- Bilingual displays around the room, which include different scripts and languages
- Bilingual labels to help newcomers
- Appropriate books in foreign languages with language tapes and pictures of the country in which the language is spoken

SKILL 9.5 **Techniques for teaching English-language learners strategies to become more independent** *(e.g., using dictionaries, using context clues, self-editing)*

Schumm claims that instruction in using dictionaries is usually deficient. Often it is limited to having students look up definitions in their dictionaries and then write the definitions in their own words. Miller and Gildea (1987 in Schumm) found the practice instructionally useless because of the numerous errors made by the children. These specific skills are critical to understanding how to use the dictionary:

- Locating words in alphabetical order
- Locating and understanding entries, including the abbreviations, synonyms, illustrations, etymology, and phrases that accompany the entry
- Matching the dictionary entries with the proper context for the target words
- Selecting the correct word among the homographs
- Pronouncing the unfamiliar words by using the diacritical marks
- Finding the correct variant part of speech

When reading, the accomplished reader takes into account the context clues available in the text. There are three types of context clues:

- Syntactic clues, which include grammatical hints, word order, word endings, and the function of words in a phrase, sentence, or passage
- Semantic clues come from within the sentence or whole text and help shed meaning on the passage
- Phonemes and graphemes, which may help in deciphering words and, therefore, meaning

ELLs can self-edit their work after completing a written assignment or a reading assignment. This involves revising their work according to the guidelines stated by the teacher, as well as reviewing their own knowledge of the grammatical system, spelling rules, and other knowledge of English that they may possess.

DOMAIN IV
ASSESSMENT

PERSONALIZED STUDY PLAN

KNOWN MATERIAL/ SKIP IT

COMPETENCY 10
KNOWLEDGE OF TESTS AND STANDARDS

SKILL
10.1 **Individual and group literacy assessments**

Teachers have the responsibility to prepare their students for and apply assessments within the classroom. Most states and school districts select appropriate tests for their students that are administered on specific days and supervised by outside personnel so that bias does not affect the results.

Some of the tests available are:

- State mandated tests, including:

  - Florida Comprehensive Assessment Test (FCAT)

  - California English Language Development Test (CELDT)

  - World-Class Instructional Design and Assessment (WIDA) in Georgia

- Commercial tests, including:

  - An Observation Survey of Early Literacy Achievement (Heinemann)

  - Bader Reading and Language Inventory (Prentice Hall)

  - Basic Early Assessment of Reading—BEAR (Riverside)

  - Brigance Comprehensive Inventory of Basic Skills (Curriculum Associates)

  - Clinical Evaluation of Language Fundamentals—CELF (Harcourt Assessment)

  - Developmental Reading Assessment—DRA (Pearson)

  - Iowa Test of Basic Skills (Riverside)

  - Stanford Diagnostic Reading Test (PsychCorp, Harcourt Assessment)

  - Wechsler Individual Achievement Test—II (Harcourt Assessment)

SKILL 10.2 National requirements regarding ESL students' identification, assessment, placement, and exit from language-support programs

Title 1 (1965) is a federal program providing funds to states to support extra assistance to students who need help in reading and mathematics.

The No Child Left Behind Act (2001), formerly the Elementary and Secondary Education Act, or ESEA, established guidelines for classifying ELLs who are entering new schools. Not all states have applied the guidelines in the same way, but the following procedures are typical.

ESL students are identified by standardized assessment tests based on a number of factors. Students entering a school for the first time must be given an assessment test of language ability (and their parents notified of the results) usually within the first thirty days of the commencement of school. If a student is deemed eligible for ESL services, the ELL begins receiving supplementary language services and is retained in the program until he/she is deemed Fully English Proficient. These students may receive a one-time, one-year deferment from the standardized testing the school is required to report for the purposes of No Child Left Behind legislation.

Each student must be assessed annually in grades 3–8 in math and reading/language arts and at least once again in grades 9-12.

For more detailed information, see Skill 14.3.

SKILL 10.3 Methods, both formal and informal, to assess productive and receptive language skills and progress

See Skill 10.6

SKILL 10.4 Identifying, selecting, and/or developing assessments to determine English-language learners' language skills

A multitude of tests exist for evaluating, assessing, and placing of ELLs in appropriate programs. Each test can test a narrow range of language skills (such as discrete tests designed to measure grammar sub-skills or vocabulary).

Language tests should be chosen on the basis of the information they give, their appropriateness for the purpose, and the soundness of their test content. Language has over 200 dimensions that can be evaluated, and yet most tests assess less than 12 of them. Therefore, all language testing should be done cautiously, backed up by teacher observations, oral interviews, family life variables, and school records.

Language placement tests

A **LANGUAGE PLACEMENT TEST** is designed to place a student within a specific program. The school district may design its own instrument or use a standardized test.

Language proficiency tests

A **LANGUAGE PROFICIENCY TEST** measures how well students have met certain standards in a particular language. The standards have been predetermined and are unrelated to any course of study, curriculum, or program. These tests are frequently used to enter or exit a particular program.

Examples are:
- *ACTFL Oral Proficiency Interview (OPI)*
- *Test of English for International Communication (TOEIC)*
- *Test of English as a Foreign Language (TOEFL)*
- *Foreign Service Exam (FSI)*
- *Oral Language Proficiency Scale from Miami-Dade County Public Schools*

Diagnostic language tests

A **DIAGNOSTIC LANGUAGE TEST** is designed to identify individual students' strengths and weaknesses in languages. They are generally administered by speech therapists or psychologists in clinical settings when specific language learning problems are present.

SKILL 10.5 **Assessments that measure English-language learners' progress toward meeting state and national standards**

Language Achievement Tests

A **LANGUAGE ACHIEVEMENT TEST** is related directly to a specific curriculum or course of study. The test includes language sub-skills, reading comprehension, parts of speech, and other mechanical parts of the language such as spelling, punctuation, and paragraphing.

> Language has over 200 dimensions that can be evaluated, and yet most tests assess less than 12 of them. Therefore, all language testing should be done cautiously, backed up by teacher observations, oral interviews, family life variables, and school records.

LANGUAGE PLACEMENT TEST: designed to place a student within a specific program

LANGUAGE PROFICIENCY TEST: measures how well students have met certain predetermined standards in a particular language

DIAGNOSTIC LANGUAGE TEST: designed to identify individual students' strengths and weaknesses in languages

LANGUAGE ACHIEVEMENT TEST: related directly to a specific curriculum or course of study

> *Examples are:*
> • *Unit exams*
> • *Final exams*

See also Skill 10.1

SKILL 10.6 **Formal and informal techniques that may be used to assess students' content-area learning at varying levels of language and literacy development**

Formal Assessment Techniques

Formal assessment techniques are used to evaluate students in content areas and in language skills. Most states have standardized tests that are given to all students at intervals throughout the year.

> *Students are being tested for many reasons other than to find out who needs remedial work. They are tested in order to exit high school, for school districts to receive federal and state funds, and to "grade" schools' performances.*

"High stakes" testing has raised the bar. Students are being tested for many reasons other than to find out who needs remedial work. They are tested in order to exit high school, for school districts to receive federal and state funds, and to "grade" schools' performances. For the student, these tests can be trying. In some cases, states are refusing to allow students who do not pass these "exit exams" to graduate.

Informal Techniques

The following are examples of alternative assessments that offer options for an instructor who wishes to informally assess students or use multiple methods of assessment.

ALTERNATIVE ASSESSMENTS	
Portfolio	A portfolio is a collection of the student's work over a period of time (report cards, creative writing, drawing, and so on); it also functions as an assessment, because it • Indicates a range of competencies and skills • Is representative of instructional goals and academic growth
Conferencing	This assessment tool allows the instructor to evaluate a student's progress or decline. Students also learn techniques for self-evaluation.

Continued on next page

Oral Interviews	Teachers can use oral interviews to evaluate the language the students are using or their ability to provide content information when asked questions—both of which have implications for further instructional planning.
Teacher Observation	During this type of assessment, the instructor observes the student behavior during an individual or group activity. Before the observation occurs, the instructor may want to create a numerical scale to rate desired outcomes.
Documentation	Documentation is similar to teacher observations, but documentation tends to take place over a period of time rather than as isolated observations.
Interviews	This type of assessment allows instructors to evaluate the student's level of English proficiency, as well as identify potential problem areas that may require correctional strategies.
Self-Assessment	Students benefit tremendously from a self-assessment, because through the process of self-analysis they begin to think for themselves. Instructors need to provide guidance as well as the criteria related to success.
Student Journals	Students benefit from journals because they are useful for keeping records as well as promoting an inner dialogue.
Story or Text Retelling	Students respond orally and can be assessed on how well they describe events in the story or text as well as their response to the story and/or their language proficiency.
Experiments and/or Demonstrations	Students complete an experiment or demonstration and present it through an oral or written report. Students can be evaluated on their understanding of the concept, explanation of the scientific method, and/or their language proficiency.
Constructed-Response Items	Students respond in writing to open-ended questions. This method focuses on how students apply information rather than on how much they recall of content lessons. In this assessment, they may use a semantic map, a brief comment on a couple of points made in the readings, or an essay discussing or evaluating the material.

SKILL 10.7 Preparing English-language learners to use self- and peer-assessment techniques

Assessing their own work is important to students because it allows them to reflect, redirect their work, and confirm their learning (O'Malley and Pierce, 1996). As students construct new knowledge, they need to be apprised of the performance standards to which they will be held accountable. ELLs need support while they are learning the process of self-evaluation. This includes plenty of practice in the skills being evaluated.

Assessing their own work is important to students because it allows them to reflect, redirect their work, and confirm their learning.

O'Malley and Pierce (1996) report that teachers can help the students evaluate their own work by:

- Discussing the elements of good oral production, reading comprehension, writing, problem solving, and working in groups.

- Providing examples (both good and bad) from previous students

- Asking students to identify characteristics of excellent work

- Giving mini-lessons on work that needs to be improved

ELLs need to practice peer assessment with a partner. The two team members can use a reference card to the rubrics of the task at hand to evaluate the strengths and weaknesses of the assignments (or a part thereof). After reviewing each other's work together, each partner corrects his or her assignment.

COMPETENCY 11
APPROPRIATE USES OF TESTS

SKILL 11.1 Accommodations for students with limited English proficiency

For ELLs, cultural and linguistic biases exist in testing. The unfortunate result may be that their true level of English proficiency and/or achievement in various content areas is incorrectly reported.

When any learners are tested, the main goal is to gather the information necessary for providing them with the most appropriate instruction. For ELLs, cultural and linguistic biases exist in testing. The unfortunate result may be that their true level of English proficiency and/or achievement in various content areas is incorrectly reported. Not only is this problematic for the ELL himself/herself, but school districts must test learners in order to comply with federal legislation, also known as "Title 1" or T1. Low test scores can sometimes result in a loss of funding for the school.

The typical guideline for testing ELLs is that they "be tested with certain minor accommodations…"

The final decision of when to test and with what accommodations should be made based on each individual ELL.

The following guidelines are accommodations for testing ELLs with at least 1 year in the T1 environment:

- Give additional time for the ELL to complete the test

- Give permission for the use of a bilingual dictionary

- Read specific parts of the test, as necessary (this accommodation is not appropriate for vocabulary or reading comprehension parts)

- Provide pronunciation and word meaning help

These accommodations are offered to the ELL so that any deficit in the T1 will not cause inaccurate performance results.

SKILL 11.2 ESL students and special education and/or gifted and talented services and referring individuals

Identification of Special Education Needs in the ESOL Student Population

Some of the characteristics of ELLs seem to be the same characteristics as those with learning disabilities. This has resulted in an over-representation of ELLs in the exceptional groupings (Ortiz & Garcia, 1995). While learning another language, students may show apparent processing difficulties, behavioral differences, reading difficulties, and expressive difficulties (Lock & Layton, 2002). Only careful observation can determine if these are natural language learning difficulties or, in fact, learning disabilities.

Before students are referred to special education classes, their previous learning experiences should be analyzed using ESOL techniques. Also, any interventions should be documented and implemented for up to ten weeks (Burnette, 1998; Rodriguez and Carrasquillo, 1997). The analysis of the results of early intervention strategies should make allowances for typical second language difficulties (Almandos and Petzold, 2001).

All exceptional students must have an Individualized Education Plan (IEP) developed in a meeting of the local education agency (LEA), special education teacher(s), general education teacher(s), someone to interpret assessment information, the parents, and the student (when appropriate). This IEP is a legally binding document for both the school and any teacher working with the student.

All exceptional students must have an Individualized Education Plan (IEP), which is a legally binding document for both the school and any teacher working with the student.

Because of the multitude of exceptionalities, it is not practical to detail all possible instructional strategies in this guide. Specific instructions for dealing with an individual's exceptionality should be spelled out in the IEP.

If no two students are alike, then no two students learn in the same way. Certain strategies may be mentioned as good teaching practices for all teachers, however, especially those dealing with exceptional students.

TEACHING PRACTICES TO USE WITH EXCEPTIONAL STUDENTS:
Teachers should use multiple instructional and assessment strategies to ensure that each student has the opportunity to learn.
Lectures are efficient methods of transferring large amounts of information, but are limited to only one sense—hearing. Combine lectures with other instructional strategies.
Objectives should be centered on students' interests and be relevant to their lives to maintain motivation.
Differentiated instruction may be used to help all students achieve their maximum potential. Differentiated instruction encompasses content, process, product, and assessment.
Students may need to prepare for test taking, because this is a stressful activity for many ELLs. Teachers can give practice timed tests, provide study guides, leave ample space for easier reading, reduce the number of choices on multiple choice tests, use cloze tests, give a selection of choices for blank spaces in tests, give students partial outlines for essay tests, and gradually reduce the amount of scaffolding for successful students.

Teachers should be able to recognize certain characteristics as possible signs of giftedness in ELLs so that when one or more of these characteristics are present to a significant degree the student is referred for screening and possible evaluation.

The following characteristics are often seen among students who are intellectually advanced ELLs:

- Successful history in previous school setting

- Advanced developmental history based on information provided in parent/guardian interview

- Rapidity of learning

- Ability to solve problems that are not dependent on English (e.g., putting complex pieces together to make a whole, sorting according to complex attributes, or doing mathematical calculations)

- High academic performance in tasks using heritage language

- Successful history in environments where heritage language is required

Exceptional students may have the added necessity of learning a new language. The Individuals with Disabilities Education Act (IDEA) does not provide funding and services for gifted programs, but leaves these programs up to the individual states.

SKILL 11.3 Assessment-related issues such as validity, reliability, language and cultural bias, and scoring concerns

Certain factors may affect the assessment of ELLs who are not familiar with assessment in the U.S. Among these is unfamiliarity with standard testing techniques. Students may become disconcerted when they are not allowed to ask questions of the teacher, are restricted by time constraints, or are not permitted to work on certain sections of the test at a given time.

Other students may also be uncomfortable when ELLs are allowed specific accommodation during the test session. Accommodations allowed by the test publisher or those prescribed by the state need to be introduced in the regular classroom so that ELLs and other students are familiar with them before the testing session begins.

> *Accommodations allowed by the test publisher or those prescribed by the state need to be introduced in the regular classroom, so that ELLs and other students are familiar with them before the testing session begins.*

The constructs of reliability and validity are crucial in assessing ELLs because of the high stakes involved in testing in today's schools. Decisions about schools, teachers, and students are based on these tests. A reliable assessment test for ELLs will have the following three attributes: validity, reliability and practicality.

Validity

An assessment test can be considered valid only if it measures what it asserts to measure. If an ELL assessment test claims to measure oral proficiency, then the test should include a section where instructors ask the ELL to pronounce certain words, listen to the instructor's pronunciation and determine if it is correct, and/or respond directly to the instructor's questions.

According to Diaz-Rico and Weed (1995), "...empirical validity is a measure of how effectively a test relates to some other known measure." There are different types of validity: predictive and concurrent (Diaz-Rico & Weed, 1995). **PREDICTIVE EMPIRICAL VALIDITY** is concerned with the possible outcomes of test performance, and **CONCURRENT EMPIRICAL VALIDITY** is connected with another

> **PREDICTIVE EMPIRICAL VALIDITY:** concerns the possible outcomes of test performance

> **CONCURRENT EMPIRICAL VALIDITY:** connected with another variable for measurement

variable for measurement. For example, if a learner shows a high level of English speech proficiency in class, then the instructor would have the expectation that the learner would perform well during an oral proficiency exam.

Avalos (in Schumm, *Reading Assessment and Instruction for All Learners*, 2006) states there are four types of bias that can affect validity:

- Cultural bias: Cultural bias concerns knowledge acquired from participating in and sharing certain cultural values and experiences. Asking questions about birthdays or holiday celebrations presumes a middle-class family experience. Immigrants frequently do not celebrate birthdays because they live in poverty or perhaps because they celebrate the birthday differently (e.g., with an extended family and *piñatas*).

- Attitudinal bias: This type of bias refers to the negative attitude of the examiner towards a certain language, dialect, or culture. Just as low expectations from instructors can cause low results in classroom performance (the Pygmalion effect), the same thing happens during testing when a negative attitude is conveyed by the assessor, teacher, or school culture. A negative attitude can result in lower (negative) test results.

- Test bias or norming bias: This type of bias refers to excluding ELLs or different populations from the school's population that is used to obtain the norm results.

- Translation bias: This type of bias occurs when the test is literally translated from L2 to L1 by interpreters or other means. The "essence" of the test may be lost in such translation because it is difficult to translate cultural concepts.

Reliability

An assessment test can only be considered reliable if similar scores result when the test is taken a second time. Factors such as anxiety, hunger, fatigue, and uncomfortable environmental conditions should not cause a huge fluctuation in the learner's score. Typically, if a learner earns a score of 90% on a test that was created by the instructor, then averages predict that the learner probably scored 45% of the points on one half of the test and 45% of the points on the other half, regardless of the structure of the test items.

Practicality

A test that proves to be both valid and reliable may unfortunately prove to be cost- or time-prohibitive. The ideal assessment test would be one that is easy to administer and easy to grade, as well as one that includes testing items similar to what the learners have experienced in class. When learners encounter test items

A test that proves to be both valid and reliable may unfortunately prove to be cost- or time-prohibitive.

such as writing journals, however, practicality becomes an issue. A writing journal, although an excellent method for learners to explore their critical literacy skills and track language achievement progress, can be difficult to grade due to the subjective content, and may it not be a fair representation of what the learners have encountered in class.

Scoring

The scoring of ELLs' performance on state-mandated, norm-referenced tests has become an issue, in part, because of the NCLB Act 2001. ELL children are disproportionately low-income and more likely to attend lower-resourced schools (Neill, 2005). Therefore, they frequently begin behind (and rarely catch up) in the "adequate yearly progress" (AYP) reports required by the Act. In previous years, schools did not worry very much about this fact. High-stakes testing, however, has made this a very important issue in the statistics reported by schools, school districts, and states that are competing for federal funds under the revised Elementary and Secondary Education Act (ESEA).

ELL children are disproportionately low-income and more likely to attend lower-resourced schools. Therefore, they frequently begin behind (and rarely catch up) in the "adequate yearly progress" reports required by the NCLB Act.

SKILL 11.4 **Norm-referenced and criterion-referenced assessments and how to use them with English-language learners**

NORM-REFERENCED TESTS are those tests in which the results are interpreted based on the performance of a given group, the norm. The norm group is a large group of individuals who are similar to the group being tested. Norm-referenced test results may be compared with the norm group using the mean and standard deviations or may be reported based solely upon the actual group being tested. The latter is referred to as grading on the curve.

CRITERION-REFERENCED TESTS are those in which the individual's test score is based on the mastery of course content. In this type of testing, it is possible for all participants to receive the highest score regardless of how many students achieve this grade.

Another category of testing refers to the first, second, and third generation language tests. The **FIRST GENERATION TESTS** approximate the grammar-translation approach to teaching language, where the student is asked to perform tasks (e.g., write an essay, answer multiple choice questions). Such questions are typically devoid of context and are not authentic. **SECOND GENERATION TESTS (TRADITIONAL TESTS)** are based on discrete points, are typically very long, and many of the items may have no connection with each other.

NORM-REFERENCED TESTS: tests in which the results are interpreted based on the performance of a given group, the norm

CRITERION-REFERENCED TESTS: tests in which the individual's test score is based on the mastery of course content

FIRST GENERATION TESTS: approximate the grammar-translation approach to teaching language, where the student is asked to perform tasks

Second generation tests are often criticized precisely because of a lack of integrative language. **THIRD GENERATION TESTS (PERFORMANCE-BASED TESTS)** are based upon the communicative principles and, by their very nature, are authentic. Examples would be listening to an airport announcement to find the time of arrival of a particular flight or writing notes from an authentic reading. The nature of the tasks requires the students to use language in an integrative form.

The strengths and weaknesses of the second and third generation tests make them suitable for different testing purposes.

COMPETENCY 12
INTERPRETING AND APPLYING ASSESSMENT RESULTS

SKILL 12.1 Using assessment results to plan and differentiate instruction

Teachers can use the results of student assessments to modify and differentiate instruction with all students. When students do not reach the standards, teachers need to look carefully at the work and decide exactly what needs to be re-taught, if necessary, and how. Reteaching a skill often can be achieved by incorporating it into the next task being taught without any undue emphasis. It is also possible that the standard was not reached because the material was too complex for the students and needs to be simplified.

It may be that the students did not have sufficient background on the topic. In some cases, a failed standard may be one of a series of standards a student has failed to meet, and consideration should be given to the necessity of initiating the process of intervention on behalf of the student. Only the teacher can analyze the assessment and set new goals for future success.

DIFFERENTIATED INSTRUCTION helps teachers cope with diverse learning and learners in the classroom. Differentiated instruction implies that teachers decide what all students will learn about a topic, what some will learn, and what a few will learn. Students are not placed in learning levels, but instead the instruction is organized so that all students have the opportunity to explore the topic. Upper levels of mastery are more complex and may be achieved by those who are eager to gain a deeper understanding of the task and material. Since all materials are available to all students, the student is in charge of the learning and the teacher becomes a facilitator or coach.

Teachers can use scaffolding techniques with ELLs by helping the learner focus on the key parts of an assignment. Through questioning, teachers provide opportunities for students to verbalize what they know (or demonstrate what they do not know) about the task. Tasks can also be broken down into smaller segments, which helps students think and talk about the task more successfully.

> With differentiated instruction, since all materials are available to all students, the student is in charge of the learning and the teacher becomes a facilitator or coach.

SKILL 12.2 Using assessment results to inform a variety of decisions (e.g., placement, advancement, exit)

Different states have different tests for the evaluation of their incoming students. Based upon the results of these tests, students may be classified as ELLs who are fully proficient in the English language or as those needing supplementary language services. Once a student is classified as an ELL, annual testing is given to monitor the progress of the student in English language learning and for possible reclassification (advancement) or exiting the program.

When students are being considered for reclassification or exiting the program, other measures are considered, such as the student's performance in basic skills, teacher evaluations, and parent or guardian opinion and consultation.

SKILL 12.3 Interpreting and communicating the results of assessments to English-language learners and their parents

The No Child Left Behind Act (2001) has mandated increased communication with parents about their children and the rights of both the parents and children. Parents must be informed of:

- The Annual Yearly Progress (AYP) of their school
- School designation information
- Pertinent information concerning Title 1 parents
- Pertinent information regarding ELLs

This information must be in the native language when possible if the parents are not speakers of English.

In addition, the NCLB act urges additional parent involvement. Parents are encouraged to be part of planning and goal-setting processes.

DOMAIN V
CULTURAL AND PROFESSIONAL ASPECTS OF THE JOB

PERSONALIZED STUDY PLAN

KNOWN MATERIAL/ SKIP IT

PERSONALIZED STUDY PLAN

KNOWN MATERIAL/ SKIP IT

PAGE	COMPETENCY AND SKILL	
	15.6: Techniques for collaboration with paraprofessionals, classroom/content-area teachers, and other instructional staff who work with English-language learners	☐
	15.7: Awareness that English-language learners and their families may have a need for a variety of outside resources	☐
	15.8: Integrating the feedback of parents/caregivers in instructional planning and decision making	☐
	15.9: Strategies for consulting with parent/caregivers and communicating with them about students' progress and needs	☐
121	**16: Professional development**	☐
	16.1: Locating information on relevant research, practice, and issues pertaining to the education of English-language learners	☐
	16.2: Organizations and publications relevant to the field of ESL	☐
	16.3: Knowing the importance of pursuing opportunities to grow in the field of ESL	☐

COMPETENCY 13
CULTURAL UNDERSTANDING

SKILL 13.1 Relationships between language and culture

While there is a continuous effort to establish a "Standard English" to be taught to English Language Learners (ELLs), English learning and acquisition depends on the cultural and linguistic background of the ELL, as well as preconceived perceptions of English language cultural influences. These factors can act as a filter, causing confusion and inhibiting learning. Since language by definition is an attempt to share knowledge, the cultural, ethnic, and linguistic diversity of learners influences both their own history and how they approach and learn a new language.

Teachers must assess the ELL to determine how cultural, ethnic, and linguistic experience can impact the student's learning. This evaluation should take into account many factors, including:

- The cultural background and educational sophistication of the ELL

- The exposure of the ELL to various English language variants and cultural beliefs

No single approach, program, or set of practices fits all students' needs, backgrounds, and experiences. The ideal program for a Native American teenager attending an isolated tribal school may fail to reach a Latino youth enrolled in an inner-city or suburban district.

Culture encompasses the sum of human activity and symbolic structures that have significance and importance for a particular group of people. Culture is manifested in language, customs, history, arts, beliefs, institutions and other representative characteristics, and is a means of understanding the lives and actions of people.

> Culture encompasses the sum of human activity and symbolic structures that have significance and importance for a particular group of people.

Customs play an important part in language learning because they directly affect interpersonal exchanges. What is polite in one culture might be offensive in another. For example, in the U.S., making direct eye contact is considered polite. Refusing to make eye contact connotes deviousness, inattention, or rude behavior. The custom in many Asian cultures is exactly the opposite. Teachers who are unaware of this cultural difference can easily offend an Asian ELL and unwittingly create a barrier to learning. Teachers who are familiar with this custom can make efforts not to offend the learner and can teach the difference between the two customs so that the ELL can learn how to interact without allowing contrary customs to interfere.

Beliefs and institutions have a strong emotional influence on ELLs and should always be respected. While customs should be adaptable, similar to switching registers when speaking, no effort should be made to change the beliefs or institutional values of an ELL. Encountering new ideas is a part of growth, learning, and understanding. Even though the beliefs and values of different cultures often have irreconcilable differences, they should be addressed. In these instances, teachers must respect alternative attitudes and adopt an "agree to disagree" attitude. Presenting new, contrasting points of view should not be avoided, because new ideas can strengthen original thinking as well as change it. All presentations should be neutral, however, and no effort should be made to alter a learner's thinking. While addressing individual cultural differences, teachers should also teach tolerance of all cultures. This is especially important in a culturally diverse classroom, but it will serve all students well in their future interactions.

While customs should be adaptable, similar to switching registers when speaking, no effort should be made to change the beliefs or institutional values of an ELL.

Studying the history and various art forms of a culture reveals much about the culture and offers opportunities to tap into the interests and talents of ELLs. Comparing the history and art of different cultures encourages critical thinking and often reveals commonalities as well as differences, leading to greater understanding among people.

If an ELL's family is supportive and embraces the second culture, the effect is typically positive; but if acculturation is perceived as rejecting the primary culture, then the child risks feeling alienated from both cultures.

Culture constitutes a rich component of language learning. It offers a means of drawing learners into the learning process and greatly expands their understanding of a new culture, as well as their own. Second language acquisition, according to the findings of Saville-Troike (1986), places the learner in the position of having to learn a "second culture." The outcome of learning a second culture can have negative or positive results, depending not only upon how teaching is approached, but also upon outside factors. How people in the new culture respond to ELLs can make them feel welcome or rejected. The attitudes and behavior of the learner's family are particularly important. If the family is supportive and embraces the second culture, the effect is typically positive; but if acculturation is perceived as rejecting the primary culture, then the child risks feeling alienated from both cultures.

Cultural variables *(e.g., individualism versus collectivism, high context or low context in language, meaning of nonverbal behaviors)* **that affect second-language acquisition and teaching and students' identities**

Cultural variables affect second-language acquisition and teaching in ways that are often imperceptible to the individuals involved. Individuals are frequently unaware that their behavior is different from that of other people. In the study of languages and culture, it is important to recognize the following observations made by researchers.

Individualism vs Collectivism

In general, students who have teachers from their culture will have less difficulty understanding the teacher's instructions than those from different cultures. When addressing a multicultural classroom, the teacher will want to plan activities that further academic and linguistic knowledge in such a way that the students will respond positively. Thus, teachers need to be aware of their teaching style and provide a variety of activities in different modes so that all cultures have the opportunity to experience education in a familiar way. For example: Latinos are generally auditory learners, Asian students are highly visual learners, and other non-Western cultures learn through tactile and kinesthetic modes (Zainuddin 2007).

In the multicultural classroom, different cultures will react differently with respect to conformity and individuality. The teacher can accommodate different styles by arranging group work in such a way that each member is held accountable for a specific task within the group (Unrau 2008).

Different cultures respond differently to cooperation and competition. For example: Muslims, Native Americans, and Asians value cooperation and loyalty to the group. They prefer not competing with others. Activities emphasizing non-competitive group results will probably work better with these students.

In many cultures, teachers are the absolute authority. In others, children are expected to respect their elders and not to disagree with them. These cultural mores may cause problems in a classroom if the teacher uses activities such as debates or asks a student to defend his position on a topic.

> *In many cultures, teachers are the absolute authority. In others, children are expected to respect their elders and not to disagree with them.*

Over the course of the school year, teachers can introduce distinctive activities in which the students have refused to participate previously by focusing on the reward, the materials, the situation, or the task requirements (Zainuddin 2007). In this way, the student is gradually introduced to a wider array of learning experiences while having support from previously successful activities.

High Context vs. Low Context in Language

These terms were made popular by the anthropologist Edward Hall (1976) in his book *Beyond Culture*. The terms refer to a culture's tendency to use high-context messages over low-context messages in daily communication. HIGH CONTEXT CULTURES prefer in-groups which leave many things unsaid because they are culturally implicit. Words and word choices are extremely important as a complex message can be communicated with few words to the insiders. A LOW CONTEXT CULTURE needs to be more explicit when communicating, and individual word choice is less important.

> **HIGH CONTEXT CULTURES:** prefer in-groups which leave many things unsaid because they are culturally implicit; words and word choices are extremely important

> **LOW CONTEXT CULTURE:** needs to be more explicit when communicating, and individual word choice is less important

Copeland and Griggs (1986) classified cultures as:

Lower context cultures	Higher context cultures
• German	• French Canadian
• American	• French
• English	• Russian
• Australian	• Italian
• English Canadian	• Spanish
	• Latin American
	• Greek
	• Arab
	• Chinese
	• Japanese

Nonverbal Behaviors

> Cultures have different nonverbal behaviors. Nodding the head means "yes" in English, but "no" in Greek.

Cultures have different nonverbal behaviors. Nodding the head means "yes" in English, but "no" in Greek. In many Latin American countries, a person's height is measured by extending the hand as if you were going to shake hands. In the United States, height is measured by extending the hand, palm down. Animals are measured this way in Spanish-speaking countries. Teachers must take care not to offend students of other cultures. When possible, these differences should be explained to all the students in the classroom in order to contribute to multicultural understanding.

SKILL 13.3 Is aware that teaching and learning styles vary across cultures

Teachers are both participants and observers in their classrooms. As such, they are in a unique position to observe what makes their students uncomfortable. By writing these observations in a teaching journal, the teacher can begin to note what activities and topics make the students in her classroom uncomfortable. Does this discomfort come from cultural insensitivity?

Anther method of demonstrating sensitivity is to use appropriate "teacher talk" in the classroom. Wait time for student responses differs in different cultures. Students who are struggling to formulate their answers may need more time than the teacher normally gives for responding. Also, if the questions are rhetorical, students may be reluctant to answer them, because they see no point to such a question.

Cooperative group work is based on the premise that many cultures are more comfortable working in collaborative groups. Even though this is true, many students may feel that the teacher is the only academic authority in the classroom and, as such, should answer questions rather than allowing their peers to do so. Different students feel more comfortable with different instructional formats, due to both cultural and individual preferences. By balancing group work with teacher-directed instruction, both preferences can be accommodated.

Literacy and reading instruction are areas where multicultural sensitivity can be increased in the classroom regardless of the level of the students. Many immigrant children arrive in the classroom with few, if any, literacy skills. They may not have had the opportunity to go to school. Others may be fully literate, with substantial prior education. In both cases, reading materials that are culturally sensitive are necessary for the students, both native English speakers and ELLs, to have the opportunity to discuss the ways in which different cultures are alike and different. Oral discussion of books will provide opportunities for input and negotiation of meaning.

Research has shown that the key to any reading program is extensive reading (Day and Bamford, 1998; Krashen, 1993). Advantages include building vocabulary and background knowledge, interest in reading, and improved comprehension. For the multicultural classroom, it is important to provide culturally sensitive materials. Avoid materials which distort or omit certain historical events, portray stereotypes, contain loaded words, use speech that is culturally offensive, portray gender roles, elders, and family inaccurately, or distort or offend a student's self-image. All materials should be of high literary quality.

> Teachers are both participants and observers in their classrooms. As such, they are in a unique position to observe what makes their students uncomfortable.

Show and Tell is another strategy for raising multicultural sensitivity. Students of all ages can bring in objects from their home cultures and tell the class about their uses, where they are from, how they are made, and so on.

Misunderstandings can be worked into the classroom by asking students to share an incident that involved cultural misunderstanding. Questions can be asked about the nature of the misunderstanding, such as what was involved: words, body language, social customs, or stereotypes.

Visual/holistic versus verbal/linear-sequential: Not all learners learn in the same manner. Some students learn best through seeing information—whether written text, charts, pictures, or flow charts. Other students prefer to hear the message spoken by a teacher or other students. Still other students learn best through tactile experiences, e.g., manipulating objects or equipment, creating models, or presenting material through art or drama.

> **HOLISTIC-ANALYTICAL LEARNER:** tends to process information either as a whole (holistic) or broken down into parts (analytic)

The **HOLISTIC-ANALYTICAL LEARNER** tends to process information either as a whole (holistic) or broken down into parts (analytic). Riding and Cheema (1991) determined that the holistic-analytical learner is commonly associated with the following terms: analytic-deductive, rigorous, constrained, convergent, formal, critical, and synthetic. The **VERBALIZER-IMAGER** tends to represent information either as words or as images.

> **VERBALIZER-IMAGER:** tends to represent information either as words or as images

Teachers need to be aware of the different ways in which students learn so that they can prepare classroom experiences and material which encompass the different learning styles. By presenting materials through different multisensory channels, all students are given an opportunity to learn material through their preferred learning style and to have it reinforced in other ways.

SKILL 13.4 Incorporating the diverse cultures of students into instruction

A culturally inclusive classroom and school environment is achieved only by those who study the cultures of their students. By observing the following suggestions, teachers can initiate a culturally aware classroom:

- Review the textbooks used in your classroom. Observe the roles of the males, females, people of color, and ethnic minorities. Do the roles seem just? Comment on inequities.

- Analyze the nonverbal communication you use and focus on teaching your students what they mean.

- Communicate respect and sincere interest in your students and their cultures.

- Make sure your classroom sends a positive, welcoming message.

- Encourage home/school interaction. Attend cultural celebrations in your students' communities.

- Make sure you are assessing content and not only language ability.

- Avoid using children as interpreters for their parents. (This may invert the normal parental hierarchy, robbing parents of their authority.)

- Understand the cultural conflict between the dominant school culture and the minority home culture.

- Encourage parents to continue speaking their native language in the home.

(Adapted from Zainuddin, 2007)

SKILL 13.5 Implications of cultural stereotyping in the school setting

Racism, stereotyping, and discrimination are difficult social issues to address in the classroom because they are cultural elements that die hard. Even so, teachers are charged with addressing these issues in the classroom. Timely intervention can help prevent violence and promote understanding of others. Encouraging an all-inclusive classroom climate where everyone is equal is a start. This is fairly easy when dealing with young children, but with older students, the movie *The Ron Clark Story* (2006) could be used to initiate a discussion of these themes. The movie shows how an idealistic young teacher from North Carolina deals with the problems of racism, stereotyping, and discrimination in his New York City classroom.

SKILL 13.6 Modeling positive attitudes toward second-language learners

Teachers and other members of the school must model positive attitudes towards ELLs at all times. When the students and their parents feel welcomed, they will be able to concentrate on the main goal—academic achievement.

When the students and their parents feel welcomed, they will be able to concentrate on the main goal—academic achievement.

Teachers can make their students feel welcomed in daily activities by

- Using scaffolding judiciously

- Creating a culturally rich environment

- Diversifying the literature used in the classroom so that many different cultures are represented

- Inviting parents to share their experiences with the class

- Explaining cultural differences to the best of their ability in a nonjudgmental way

- Encouraging parents to express their concerns about their children and their children's education

- Relating content subjects to the backgrounds of the students and their parents

SKILL 13.7 Cultural conflicts and other events in students' lives that have an impact on English-language learners' dispositions and learning

People know what is expected of them in their own cultures, but when different cultures come together, they do not know what they are expected to do or how to react to different situations.

People know what is expected of them in their own cultures, but when different cultures come together, they do not know what they are expected to do or how to react to different situations. Teachers should be able to bridge these situations by being culturally aware and respectful of all cultures.

Teachers who are culturally aware avoid using cultural elements that cause students embarrassment. Not only are many cultural elements of the mainstream American culture completely opposite of other cultures, some are offensive. To avoid these problems, teachers must actively study other cultures and learn about such behaviors.

By encouraging an open dialogue with parents, teachers become aware of cultural differences, such as cultures which limit the role of women in their society, encourage education and learning, permit touching or reject it, respect time or disregard it completely, are deeply religious, etc. As teachers become familiar with the cultures present in the classroom, they are more equipped to deal with cultural differences. In extreme cases, students will come to school seeking a safe haven from home problems or from the problems that caused them to become refugees. It is up to teachers to provide this safe haven.

SKILL 13.8 Factors *(e.g., parents' educational attainment, students' previous schooling, gender)* that may influence an English-language learner's language development

Social factors such as gender, social status, age, occupation, and educational level have an impact on second language acquisition. How learners perceive themselves and what opportunities are available to them influence their attitudes toward education, as well as what they are able to achieve academically.

Gender influences second language acquisition, particularly of English. Typically, families who immigrate to the United States bring with them their experience of gender roles. Parents often exert a negative attitude towards education for their children, especially girls. Depending on the country, strict cultural norms can diminish the role of the woman while placing higher value on the man. Countries such as China value males more than females. If a Chinese family immigrated to the United States, existing sexist attitudes towards the female would still prevail, regardless of the new culture's attitudes toward gender equality. As a result, the family may focus on and only be supportive of the education of their sons, placing little emphasis on their daughters' education.

Many other cultures, including many Latin American cultures, value the traditional role of women as mothers and homemakers. Many Latino families feel that education goes against what they want for their daughters and will not allow them to continue with higher education.

However, many parents are recognizing that the only way for their children to have a better life than they did is through education. They strongly encourage their children to get an elementary education and even support them through high school and college. Many of these parents make considerable sacrifices to obtain education for their children.

Previous schooling may determine the attitude of ELLs towards school. Children who have not had the opportunity for schooling may feel that they are too old for the elementary education they need and are struggling to obtain. Many drop out of school to earn money for their families. Again, there are exceptions. Many immigrant children are highly motivated and struggle silently to obtain the education they need.

See Skill 4.4, Motivation

> *Typically, families who immigrate to the United States bring with them their experience of gender roles. Parents often exert a negative attitude towards education for their children, especially girls.*

SKILL 13.9 Teacher's personal and cultural experiences that may influence teaching style

Teachers who are raised in the North American culture are considered field-independent. In general, this means that the teacher is independent, competitive, emphasizes details of concepts, and emphasizes facts and principles (Zainuddin, 2007). Students from Asian or Latino cultures are more field-sensitive. Field-sensitive cultures value assisting others, are sensitive to others' feelings, seek guidance and demonstration from the teacher, and teachers instruct primarily by modeling. If the classroom teacher is insensitive to these cultural differences, communication problems may occur in the classroom.

SKILL 13.10 Knowing how to explain United States cultural norms to English-language learners

The United States' cultural norms need to be explained to English language learners. This requires constant study as well as experience in dealing with foreign cultures. Something that is important to one culture may be seem to be totally irrelevant to a person from a different culture. (Zainuddin, 2007).

All teachers involved in the process of instructing immigrant students can help the new student adjust to the United States culture by:

- Expressing a positive attitude toward those aspects of the foreign culture that are different when they appear in the classroom

- Incorporating aspects of the diverse cultures into the classroom lessons (music, food, and dress)

- Validating the ELL's culture by visiting their homes using paraprofessionals and others (but not the child) as interpreters

- Using classroom tools such as dialogue journals, the buddy system, multicultural study groups sharing cultural mores, and fostering a welcoming attitude to smooth transition of newcomers

(Zainuddin, 2007)

Large scale migrations have caused world governments to carefully consider what is culture and cultural identity. For many ELLs entering U.S. schools, their cultural identity has been challenged by migration. Political unrest and wars, natural disasters, need for improved living conditions—all contribute to the desire of populations and individuals to migrate to other countries and cultures. In recent U.S. history, one of the most recognized periods of immigration was the third period of migrations from Cuba from December 1965 to April 1973, known as the Freedom Flights, that resulted from the fall of Batista (Beebe and Mackey, 1990). Many of these refugees were wealthy, well-educated professionals or businessmen, who, as time went on and their hopes of an early return to Cuba diminished, were forced to start or purchase modest businesses. Those without resources were forced into more menial jobs.

For many ELLs entering U.S. schools, their cultural identity has been challenged by migration.

The fall of Saigon in April 1975 led to a wave of immigration from Vietnam. Since 1975, over 650,000 Vietnamese people have left Vietnam for the U.S. Vietnamese is the seventh most commonly spoken language in the U.S. Because of strong U.S. government support of the immigration of Vietnamese to the U.S., President Gerald Ford signed the Indochina Migration and Refugee Assistance Act in 1975, and Congress passed the Refugee Act of 1980, permitting the early entry of refugees to the U.S. in response to the Vietnamese government's establishment of the Orderly Departure Program (ODP) under the United Nations High Commissioner for Refugees, in response to world protest of the former enemy combatants. According to the American Community Survey of the U.S. Census Bureau (2006), more than 1,599,394 Vietnamese live in the U.S., and more than 46% of these entered the U.S. after 1990.

These two comparatively recent historical incidents illustrate changes not only in our recent cultural history, but also in the lives of those who are forced to make decisions that drastically affect their futures and their children. In modern society, relationships are defined not only by the family, but also by the school, the workplace, the professional organization, and the church. Each organization has its own power hierarchy, its expected roles and statuses, its characteristic values and beliefs, and attitudes and ideologies (Kramsch, 1998). Geographic mobility, professional change, and life experiences may cause people to experience internal conflict due to multiple social identities.

Geographic mobility, professional change, and life experiences may cause people to experience internal conflict due to multiple social identities.

COMPETENCY 14
LEGAL AND ETHICAL ISSUES

> **SKILL 14.1** **Legal provisions and ethical implications of laws and court decisions related to the education of English-language learners** *(e.g., Castaneda v. Pickard, Title III, Lau v. Nichols)*

In 1961, due to the large numbers of Cuban children who migrated to Florida, Dade County Public Schools became one of the first school districts to put a major bilingual education program into action. In 1968, the Bilingual Education Act, now known as Title VII of the Elementary and Secondary Education Act (ESEA), was passed by Congress, which provided funding for all school districts to implement programs for LEP[1] students so that they could participate in academic activities.

Since then, the Supreme Court has ruled favorably in the following case, which legally required school districts to improve educational opportunities for LEP students.

Lau v. Nichols (1974): A 1969 class action suit filed on behalf of the Chinese community in San Francisco alleged that the school district denied "equal educational opportunity" to their children because the classes the children were required to attend were not taught in the native Chinese language. The Supreme Court ruled in favor of the plaintiffs, stating that no student shall be denied "equal access" to any academic program due to "limited English proficiency." The Court determined a set of requirements that academic programs must provide.

> The "Lau Remedies" became guidelines for all states to assist in the academic needs of LEP students; the "Lau Remedies" also provided guidelines for "exiting" LEP programs.

Related to *Lau v. Nichols*, the Office of the Department of Health, Education and Welfare created a committee of experts, who established guidelines and procedures for local educational groups serving the LEP population. The "Lau Remedies" became guidelines for all states to assist in the academic needs of LEP students; the "Lau Remedies" also provided guidelines for exiting LEP programs.

In 1998, Proposition 227 was passed in California, mandating that English learners be taught following a specific pattern. Instruction was to be "overwhelmingly in English," and students were to have immersion classes with sheltered, or

---

1 The term Limited English Proficiency (LEP) students has been replaced in common usage with English Language Learner (ELL) in most areas of English Language teaching. Nevertheless, the LEP terminology occurs in older legal documents, lawsuits, and court decisions.

structured, English instruction for a maximum of one year. Parents were given the alternative of signing a waiver if they wished their student to receive bilingual education.

Since California currently has more than one-third of the five million English learners in the United States, the proposition had great impact. After five years, the California Department of Education commissioned the American Institute for Research to conduct a study of the results of Proposition 227. The following are findings of that study:

- The performance gap between English Learners and other students remained constant over the five years of the study. This finding is significant because during the period in question there was a substantial increase in the number of ELLs participating in statewide testing.

- The likelihood of an ELL student reclassifying to English-proficient status after ten years in California schools is less than 40 percent.

- The methods recommended by Proposition 227 have been shown to have no significant impact on the success of English Learners.

The recommendation of the study was that schools put less emphasis on specific methods and focus more on rewarding academic success and implementing appropriate interventions when failure occurs (Parrish, 2006).

Section (9) of *Title III, the renewed No Child Left Behind Act,* would seem to set itself in direct opposition to Proposition 227:

(Section 3102. Purposes)

The purposes of this part are:

> (8) to hold State educational agencies, local educational agencies, and schools accountable for increases in English proficiency and core academic content knowledge of limited English proficient children by requiring:
>
>> (A) demonstrated improvements in the English proficiency of limited English proficient children each fiscal year; and
>>
>> (B) adequate yearly progress for limited English proficient children, including immigrant children and youth, as described in section 1111(b)(2)(B); and
>
> (9) to provide State educational agencies and local educational agencies with the flexibility to implement language instruction educational programs, based on scientifically based research on teaching limited English proficient children, that the agencies believe to be the most effective for teaching English.

> *It can be seen that the best policies and methods for teaching English Learners remain very much open to debate, even at the highest levels of policy making.*

SKILL 14.2 Ways in which the ESL teacher is affected by local, state, and national regulations (e.g., design and implementation of a variety of ESL programs and models)

> To a great extent, local, state, and national regulations have mandated the way in which ESOL is taught.

To a great extent, local, state, and national regulations have mandated the way in which ESOL is taught. Programs are selected based on the way in which the laws are interpreted. Parents are rightly concerned about the education their children receive and governments expect full value on the dollar. The onus of fulfilling all these many regulations fall to the school administration, and, ultimately, to the teacher.

Teachers recognize that there have been many changes since the days when students were punished for speaking their heritage language on school grounds and a new student's name was routinely translated to an English version. Yet, the legislation governing instruction of English Learners allows wide latitude for interpretation within districts and schools.

How much of the instructional day, for instance, is required to be conducted in English? What constitutes "appropriate additional support?" How is a school to provide accurate placement for students without first-language assessment materials to determine special needs? How can the school recognize and record progress in English literacy that remains well below state grade-level standards? Many of these questions are decided at the district level, making best practices difficult to identify and disseminate and allowing for a wide variance in the quality of services offered.

Collier and Thompson have researched innovative programs and conducted research in 23 school districts in 15 states for more than 14 years. (1999/2000 in Zainuddin, 2007). Based on their research, they have discovered five basic principles that apply to most programs in the field of ESOL teaching and that promote high standards for ELLs:

- Learning is facilitated through the cooperative, productive efforts of the teacher and the students.

- Language and literacy should be developed throughout all instructional activities.

- Content is contextualized using the skills and experiences of home and community.

- Students are challenged cognitively.

- Students need to be engaged in warm, instructional conversation when working on activities.

SKILL
14.3 **Legal and ethical issues related to the assessment of English-language learners**

The No Child Left Behind Act (NCLB) was signed into law on January 8, 2002 and was effective for a period of six years.

The NCLB Act requires schools to focus on providing quality education for students who are often overlooked by the educational system: children with disabilities, children from low-income families, non-English speakers, and African-Americans and Latinos. The following regulations, geared specifically for LEP students, were implemented in the latest revision:

- LEP students are required to be included in all academic assessments that are currently administered to other (non-LEP) students.

- When possible, the assessments must be administered in the language most likely to provide the most accurate data of the student's academic achievement and performance.

- When and if academic assessments in the student's native language cannot be obtained, the state is responsible for developing the appropriate assessment.

- In general, LEP students who have attended U.S. schools (except Puerto Rico) for at least three consecutive years must be administered assessments in English.

- The exception to this last regulation is the following: On an individual-case basis, schools have the option of permitting LEP students an extra two years before the school administers assessments in English, if the school has determined that the LEP student's current level of English proficiency will not provide valid data.

- Parents are to be provided with a detailed report of student achievement, including explanations of achievement levels.

Core provisions of the NCLB Act are:

- All students must be proficient in reading and math by 2014, as defined and mandated by state standards.

- States must assess students in math and reading once a year in grades 3–8 and at least once during high school.

- Every public school must be evaluated to see if it has made Adequate Yearly Progress (AYP). This is based primarily on the percentage of students scoring "proficient" or above on state assessments, overall and for each of the following categories of students: economically disadvantaged students, students from major racial and ethnic groups, students with disabilities, and students with limited English proficiency (LEP).

- Schools that receive Title I funding and are identified as "needing improvement" must develop a school improvement plan. For each year that the school does not make AYP, the school must undertake specific actions to overcome its deficiencies. These schools are required to spend federal funds to implement federally mandated strategies—public school choice, supplemental education services (SES), corrective action, and restructuring.

(Adapted from Alliance for Excellent Education, 2007)

In 2009, the American Recovery and Reinvestment Act included a program called **RACE TO THE TOP (RTT)** as a stimulus to encourage K-12 educational reform in state and local districts. States which apply for the funding are scored in different areas for a total of 500 points.

RACE TO THE TOP (RTT): American Recovery and Reinvestment Act stimulus to encourage educational reform in state and local districts (K-12)

- Great Teachers and Leaders (138 points)

- State Success Factors (125 points)

- Standards and Assessments (70 points)

- General Selection Criteria (55 points)

- Turning Around the Lowest-Achieving Schools (50 points)

- Data Systems to Support Instruction (47 Points)

- Prioritizing of STEM (science, technology, engineering, and math) (15 points)

The program has been criticized by teachers' unions and state's rights advocates who oppose federal interference in the field of education.

COMPETENCY 15
ROLE OF THE ESL TEACHER

SKILL **The connection between language instruction and content**
15.1 **instruction and English-language learners' academic success**

See Skill 7.1

SKILL 15.2 Serving as a resource and advocate for students and families

By advocating for the ELL, the ESOL instructor can ensure that the students in his or her charge are able to participate in the school band, science club, math club, chess club, sports teams, and all other activities in which students of their age and inclination participate.

Encouraging students and their families to make full use of public resources such as the local public library—including its online resources—will help them expand their own knowledge and understanding of resources available to English-language learners. In addition, many libraries have after-school, Saturday, or holiday programs to encourage constructive use of students' time.

Museums, too, often have educational outreach programs that may be used by all citizens. Other resources such as parks and the local YMCA and YWCA (or similar organizations) offer recreational facilities to all citizens.

By advocating for the ELL, the ESOL instructor can ensure that the students in his or her charge are able to participate in all the activities in which other students of their age and inclination participate.

SKILL 15.3 The need to communicate with school personnel about the characteristics and emotional/physical needs of English-language learners

The ESOL teacher is an advocate for her charges with other school personnel. She must be able to explain the emotional needs of children who are encountering a different culture, language, and school system. Some of these children may also be experiencing physical needs (e.g., visual problems or hearing problems) that need resolving.

ESOL teachers refer to the emotional needs of students as the **AFFECTIVE DOMAIN**. The term affective domain encompasses the range of feelings and emotions in human behavior that affects how a second language is acquired. Self-esteem, motivation, anxiety, and attitude all contribute to the second-language acquisition process. Internal and external factors influence the affective domain. ESOL teachers must be aware of each student's personality and stay attuned to affective factors in their students' lives.

AFFECTIVE DOMAIN: the emotional needs of ELL students

Motivation

See Skill 4.4

Inhibition

ELLs may be inhibited about trying to say things in their target language—English. They might worry about what others will think of their speech. They might be afraid of making mistakes or losing face. They may be shy about speaking in front of others.

Attitudes

Attitudes typically evolve from internalized feelings about oneself and one's ability to learn a language. On the other hand, one's attitude about a language and the speakers of that language is largely external and influenced by the surrounding environment of classmates and family.

Schools can significantly improve attitudes toward second-language learners by encouraging activities between native speakers and ELLs.

If nonnative speakers of English experience discrimination because of their accents or cultural status, their attitude toward the value of second-language learning may change. Schools can significantly improve attitudes toward second-language learners by encouraging activities between native speakers and ELLs. This can be particularly beneficial to both groups if students learning the ELL's first language work on projects together with ELLs. When native speakers get a chance to appreciate the ELL's language skill in their first language, attitudes change and ELLs have an opportunity to shine.

Anxiety

Anxiety is inherent in second-language learning. Students are required to take risks, such as speaking in front of their peers. Without a native's grasp of the language, second-language learners are less able to express their individuality, which is even more threatening and uncomfortable. Even so, not all anxiety is debilitative. Bailey's (1983) research suggests that "facilitative anxiety" (anxiety that compels an individual to stay on task) is a positive factor for some learners, closely related to competitiveness.

Self-Esteem

Using teaching techniques that decrease stress and emphasize group participation rather than focusing on getting the right answer reduces anxiety and encourages learners to attempt to use the new language.

Learning a second language puts learners in a vulnerable frame of mind. While some learners are less inhibited than others about taking risks, all learners can experience stress if forced to go beyond their comfort level. Using teaching techniques that decrease stress and emphasize group participation rather than focusing on getting the right answer reduces anxiety and encourages learners to attempt to use the new language.

Teachers' Expectations

Teachers' expectations regarding learning objectives and goals should be high for all students, including ELLs. Teachers' expectations in terms of behavior should be clearly stated and posted in the classroom.

Classroom Culture

The teacher is responsible for establishing an effective classroom community where all students feel safe, are responsible and respectful, and work cooperatively with their classmates. Students will engage in activities that are meaningful and functional. Teachers should provide demonstrations and scaffolding as needed, yet students should be encouraged to make guesses and take risks in their learning activities. The teacher should allow students to have choices about the activities in which they will be involved, e.g., in which form they will be allowed to present a book report (as a diorama, a written report, or a multimedia project).

> ### SKILL 15.4 Strategies for planning and conducting collaborative conferences with English-language learners, their families, and school/community members

Teachers who are culturally responsible use a variety of methods to involve the families and communities in the classroom and school so that student achievement is maximized. For example teachers can:

- Plan meetings at hours when working parents can attend

- Maintain a friendly main office with translation services when needed

- Invite parents to share their expertise or knowledge with the class

- Invite parents to help out in the classroom

- Call parents or send home handwritten notes (in first language) with good news about their children

- Encourage parent-to-parent communication and hotlines

- Provide school materials in the native language

- Provide handouts of parents' rights, per the Bilingual Education Act

- Create a classroom newsletter for parents

- Enter students in artistic or literary events or programs sponsored by community or professional organizations

- Encourage bilingualism as a badge of honor in school

- Help students achieve remedial aid in a timely manner

- Make meetings a social event with food and performances by students if time permits

- Give recognition to family members at award ceremonies

> **SKILL 15.5** **Strategies for involving families, school personnel, and community members in planning transitions** (e.g., grade levels, programmatic, and school-to-work) **for English-language learners**

When students are transitioning from one level of school to another, they are concerned about what to expect. For middle school students who transition to high school, the stress can be overwhelming. Some of the problems associated with this type of transition are:

- High school offers less school support to individual students

- Students experience lower grades

- School attendance suffers

- Academic motivation drops

- Mental health problems such as substance abuse, depression, and delinquency increase

Because of the gravity of the problems associated with transitioning, many schools are proactive in tackling them.

Because of the gravity of the problems associated with transitioning, many schools are proactive in tackling them. Families, school personnel, and community members work as an integrated unit to ease the difficulties middle schoolers experience. Activities associated with successful transition are:

- Visiting the new campus

- Meeting the freshman principal, counselor, activities director, and former students

- Holding a question and answer session for incoming students

- Registering at the high school

Since this process is especially difficult for ELLs and students with disabilities, careful planning must include appropriate activities and accommodations for these at-risk groups of students.

Similar planning will ease the difficulties faced by students in transitioning from one grade to another, entering the work force, and/or attending college.

SKILL 15.6 Techniques for collaboration with paraprofessionals, classroom/content-area teachers, and other instructional staff who work with English-language learners

See Skill 7.3

SKILL 15.7 Awareness that English-language learners and their families may have a need for a variety of outside resources *(e.g., services, networks, organizations)*

State and local governments provide diverse support to English language learners and their families. This support may be organized and funded under the umbrella of human departments and/or non-profit organizations, networks, and organizations that offer support to those of their race or culture. Examples of such organizations are:

- Chinese Information and Service Center
- El Centro de la Raza
- Refugee Women's Alliance
- SafeFutures Youth Center
- Youth & Family Services

These entities may partner with schools and offer support to those trying to adjust to a different culture and language.

SKILL 15.8 Integrating the feedback of parents/caregivers in instructional planning and decision making

Each school and school district has a multitude of school advisory committees for the parents of the children involved. These committees welcome parental involvement. It is the legal obligation of the teacher and the school staff to provide information to parents of all children in the school about serving on committees to improve academic achievement, formulate policies on multilingual and multicultural issues, and provide the best education possible for special needs students.

While each state and school district is different, committees such as the following welcome parental involvement:

- Autism Advisory Committee (AAC)

- Citizens' Advisory Committee for Special Education (CACSE)

- District English Learners Advisory Committee (DELAC)

- GATE Parent Advisory Committee (GAC)

- Migrant Education Parent Advisory Committee

- Parent Education/Involvement Task Force

- Parent Teacher Association/Parent Teacher Student Association Council

- School English Learners Advisory Committee (SELAC)

SKILL 15.9 Strategies for consulting with parent/caregivers and communicating with them about students' progress and needs

Strategies for consulting with parents/caregivers and communicating with them about students' progress and needs involve careful planning and preparation. Some of the strategies teachers use include:

- Creating documents that explain the teacher's grading policies to avoid conflict over this delicate subject

- Communicating the upcoming assignments, tests, field trips, and school events through a newsletter

- Developing a set of rubrics to be communicated to parents and having them sign these documents to help establish progress (or lack of) over a period of time when assignments are heavily weighted or involve multiple processes and careful organization

- Designating a folder for communications sent to and from home (emails, handwritten notes, and a log for personal and phone conferences)

COMPETENCY 16
PROFESSIONAL DEVELOPMENT

SKILL 16.1 Locating information on relevant research, practice, and issues pertaining to the education of English-language learners

Research on relevant practices and issues is often difficult to locate. The Internet offers a quick way to check facts. Locating pertinent scholarly research, however, is time-consuming and costly unless the researcher has access to a first-class data bank.

Teachers can begin with the resources listed below in Skill 16.2. Another suggestion is to enlist the aid of the nearest librarian when particular information cannot be located.

SKILL 16.2 Organizations and publications relevant to the field of ESL

Organizations that provide additional resources supplying help to educators of ELLs include:

- **Teachers of English to Speakers of Other Languages, Inc.** and its regional affiliates
  www.tesol.org

- **Bilingual Association of Florida**
  Oneyda M. Paneque, Ed.D.
  Miami Dade College
  School of Education
  P.O. Box 651182
  Miami, FL 33265
  Phone: 305-237-6707
  Fax: 305-237-6179
  Email: *opaneque@mdc.edu*
  www.nabe.org/aff_florida.html

- **Center for Applied Linguistics**
  www.cal.org

- **U.S. Department of Education's Office of English Language Acquisition Language Enhancement, and Academic Achievement for Limited English Proficient Students (OELA)**
  www.ed.gov/offices/OELA/

Books and journals offer supplemental resources for addressing cultural, ethnic, and linguistic differences; among the noteworthy are:

- **Beebe, Von N. and Mackey, William F.** *Bilingual Schooling and the Miami Experience.* Coral Gables: Institute of Interamerican Studies. Graduate School of International Studies. University of Miami, 1990. Extensively documents the influx of Cuban refugees into the Miami-Dade County school system.

  TESOL Journal

  Bilingual Research Journal

Several websites provide additional resources for teachers of ELLs:

- WebQuests
  http://webquest.sdsu.edu

  WebQuests supports teachers with a scaffold for organizing theme-based research units by using the Internet as a learning tool and source of information.

- Wiggle Works
  www.ed.gov/pubs/TechStrength/scholastic.html

  This early literacy, bilingual series incorporates universally designed CD-ROMs for each book in the database (from Scholastic and the Center for Applied Special Technology).

General resources available on the web

Besides their specific charge, these offices generally include information on ESL/bilingual educational issues, documents, and teaching resources of concern to educators across the nation. See each web site's home page for more details on their mission and services offered.

- California Department of Education
  http://www.cde.ca.gov/sp/el/

- Center for Multilingual, Multicultural Research
  http://www-rcf.usc.edu/~cmmr/

- ERIC Clearinghouse on Language and Linguistics
  http://www.eric.ed.gov

- Kristina Pfaff's Linguistic Funland
  http://www.linguistic-funland.com

- National Association for Bilingual Education
  http://www.nabe.org

- National Clearinghouse for English Language Acquisition
  http://www.ncela.gwu.edu

- Education Northwest
  http://educationnorthwest.org

- Office of Superintendent of Public Instruction (OSPI), Washington State
  http://www.k12.wa.us

- University of Texas at Austin, College of Education
  http://www.edb.utexas.edu/education/centers/obe

- The U.S. Department of Education
  http://www.ed.gov

- The Office for Civil Rights (OCR)
  http://www2.ed.gov/about/offices/list/ocr/index.html?src=oc

- Office of English Language Acquisition, Language Enhancement and
  Academic Achievement for Limited English Proficient Student
  http://www2.ed.gov/about/offices/list/oela/index.html?src=oc

- The Institute of Education Sciences
  http://www2.ed.gov/about/offices/list/ies/index.html?src=oc

Web sites are available on the Internet for students to practice their ELL skills.
Two of the most popular are:

- About.com: ESL: This popular site has exercises in all four skills, games, and
  quizzes for ELLs as well as information for teachers.
  http://www.esl.about.com

- Dave's ESL Café: One of the longest-running websites with sections for
  students, teachers, and jobs
  http://www.eslcafe.com

SKILL 16.3 Knowing the importance of pursuing opportunities to grow in the field of ESL

Professional development plans are guides to help teachers achieve their long-term and short-term goals as educators.

Professional development plans are guides to help teachers achieve their long-term and short-term goals as educators. By planning and writing down these goals, the teacher is more likely to achieve them than teachers who only keep these goals in their heads. A listing of goals, actions, and assessments will lead to a deeper understanding of the steps to be taken to achieve these goals and, at the same time, promote personal reflection.

Participation in professional associations and other academic organizations provides the opportunity for teaching professionals to connect to colleagues, receive new information about professional issues, learn about trends and research in the field, and be inspired by new ideas.

References

Alderson, J. and Beretta, A. 1992. *Evaluating second language education.* Cambridge University Press. 1992.

Ellis, R. 1997. The empirical evaluation of language teaching materials. *ELT Journal.* 51 (1) Jan.

Allen, V. G. 1994. Selecting materials for the instruction of ESL children. In: Zainuddin (2007).

Alliance for Excellent Education. 2007. Policy Brief. June. Washington, DC *www.all4ed.org.*

Lawsuit Against NCLB Renewed. 2008. *Education matters.* News from Washington, D.C. February. *www.aaeteachers.org.*

Au, K. H. 1993. *Literacy instruction in multicultural settings.* Orlando, FL.: Harcourt Brace.

————. 2002. Multicultural factors and effective instruction of students of diverse backgrounds. In: Farstrup, A., and S. J. Samuels, eds. *What research says about reading instruction.* Newark, DE: International Reading Assn. Coral Gables: Univ. of Miami. 392-413.

Banks, J. A. 1988. *Multicultural leader.* 1 (2). Educational Materials and Services Center. Spring.

Bebe, V. N., and W. F. Mackey. 1990. *Bilingual schooling and the Miami experience.* Coral Gables, FL: University of Miami. Institute of Interamerican Studies. Graduate School of International Studies.

Bennett, C. 1995. *Comprehensive multicultural education: Theory and practice.* 3rd ed. Boston: Allyn & Bacon.

Berko Gleason, J. 1993. *The development of language.* 3rd ed. New York: Macmillan.

Bialystok, E., ed. 1991. *Language processing in bilingual children.* Cambridge: Cambridge University Press.

Blakey, E., and S. Spence, 1990. Developing metacognition (ED327218). Syracuse, NY: ERIC Clearinghouse on Information Resources.

Burstall, C., M. Jamieson, S. Cohen, and M. Hargreaves. 1974. *Primary French in the balance.* Slough: NFER.

California Department of Education. Testing and Accountability. CELDT Questions and Answers. Rev. 11/03/09. *http://www.cde.ca.gov/ta/tg/el/celdtfaq.asp.*

Candlin, C. 1987. In Batstone, R. 1994. *Grammar.* Oxford: Oxford University Press.

Chamot, A. U., and J. M. O'Malley. 1994. *The Calla handbook.* Reading, MA: Addison-Wesley.

Cloud, J. 2007. Are We Failing Our Geniuses? *Time.* August 16. *http://www.time.com/magazine/article/0,9171,1653653,00.html*

Collier, V. P. 1989. How long? A synthesis of research on academic achievement in second language. *TESOL Quarterly.* 23: 509-31.

———. 1992. A synthesis of studies examining long-term language minority student data on academic achievement. *Bilingual Research Journal.* 16 (1-2): 187-212.

———. 1995. Acquiring a second language for school. *Directions in language and education.* Washington, DC: NCBE. 1(4): 1-10.

Conflict Research Consortium. Online training program on intractable conflict (OTPIC) conflict management and constructive confrontation: A guide to the theory and practice. University of Colorado. Revised July 20, 1999. *http://conflict.colorado.edu/.*

Criteria for evaluating instructional materials: Kindergarten through grade eight. reading/language arts framework for California public schools. California Department of Education. 2007.

Cummins, J. 1981. *Bilingualism and minority language children.* Toronto: Institute for Studies in Education.

Dahlgren, M. 2005. *English in the community.* Vigo: Funiber.

Diaz-Rico, L. T. 2004. *Strategies for teaching English learners.* 2nd ed. Boston: Pearson.

Diaz-Rico, L. T., and K. Z. Weed. 1995. *Language and academic development handbook: A complete K–12 reference guide.* Needham Heights, MA: Allyn & Bacon.

Dulay, H., and M. Burt. 1974. You can't learn without goofing. In: J. Richards, ed. *Error analysis, perspectives on second-language acquisition.* New York: Longman.

Ellis, R. 1985. *Understanding second-language acquisition*. Oxford: Oxford University Press.

———. 1994. *The study of second-language acquisition*. Oxford: Oxford University Press.

———. 1997. The empirical evaluation of language teaching materials. *ELT Journal*. 51 (1) Jan.

Entwhistle, N. J., and D. Entwhistle. 1970. The relationships between personality, study methods and academic performance. *British Journal of Educational Psychology*. 40(2): 132-43. doi.apa.org

Fillmore, L. W. 2001. Scott, Foresman. ESL: Accelerating English language learning. In Zainuddin (2007).

Friend, M., and W. D. Bursuck. 2005. *Including students with special needs: A practical guide for classroom teachers*. 4th ed. Boston: Allyn & Bacon.

Garcia, E. 1994. *Understanding and meeting the challenge of student cultural diversity*. Boston: Houghton Mifflin.

Garinger, D. 2002. Textbook evaluation. *TESL Web Journal*. 1(3).

Genesee, F. 1987. *Learning through two languages: Studies of immersion and bilingual education*. Cambridge, MA: Newbury House.

———, ed. 1994. *Educating second-language children: The whole child, the whole curriculum, the whole community*. Cambridge: Cambridge University Press.

Grellet, F. 1981. *Developing reading skills*. Cambridge: Cambridge University Press.

Harris, M., and P. McCann. 1994. *Assessment*. Oxford: Heinemann.

Heywood, D. 2006. Using whole-discourse tasks for language teaching. www.jalt-publications.org/tlt/chaprep/ Jan.

Hoff, D.J. 2009. National Standards Gain Steam. *Education Matters*. September. www.aaeteachers.org

Hyland, K. 2002. *Teaching and Researching Writing*. Harrow, England: Pearson.

Jerald, C. D. 2006. School culture: "The hidden curriculum." The Center for Comprehensive School Reform and Improvement. Issue Brief. December. www.centerforcsri.org

Kramsch, C. 1998. *Language and culture*. Oxford: Oxford University Press.

Krashen, S. 1985. *The Input Hypothesis*. New York: Longman.

———.1982. *Principles and practice in second language acquisition*. Oxford: Pergamon Press.

———. 1981. *Second-language acquisition and second-language learning*. Oxford: Pergamon Press.

Lambert, W., and O. Klineberg. 1967. *Children's views of foreign peoples: A crossnational study*. New York: Appleton. (Review in Shumann, J. 1975. Affective factors and the problem of age in second language acquisition. *Language Learning*. 25(2): 209-35).

Larsen, D., and W. Smalley. 1972. *Becoming bilingual: A guide to language learning*. New Canadian, CT: Practical Anthropology.

Larsen-Freeman, D. 1997. Chaos/complexity science and second language acquisition. *Applied Linguistics*.18(2): 141-65.

Lawsuit Against NCLB Renewed. 2008. *Education Matters*. News from Washington, D.C. February. *www.aaeteachers.org*.

Long, M. 1990. The lease a second language acquisition theory needs to explain. *TESOL Quarterly*. 24(4): 649-66.

Lyons, J. 1977. *Semantics*. Cambridge: Cambridge University Press.

The Map of Standards for ELS. 2002. 3rd ed. West Education.

McArthur, T., ed. 1992. *The Oxford companion to the English language*. Oxford: Oxford University Press. 571-73.

McCarthy, Michael. 1991.*Discourse analysis for language teachers*. Cambridge, England: Cambridge University Press.

McClelland, D., J. Atkinson, R. Clark, and E. Lowell. 1953. *The achievement motive*. New York: Appleton, Century, Crofts.

McDonough, J., and S. Shaw 1993. *Materials and methods in ELT: A teacher's guide*. Blackwell.

McKay, S. L. 1987. *Teaching grammar: Form, function, and technique*. New York: Prentice Hall.

McLaughlin, B. 1990. The development of bilingualism: Myth and reality. In Barona, A., and E. Garcia, eds. *Children at risk: poverty, minority status and other issues in educational equity*. Washington, DC: National Association of School Psychologists.

Menken, K. 2006. Teaching to the Test: How No Child Left Behind Impacts Language Policy, Curriculum, and Instruction for English Language Learners. *Bilingual Research Journal*, 30(2) Summer. 521-546.

Mora, J.K. 2006. Differentiating instruction for English Learners: The four-by-four model. In T.A. Young and N. L. Hadaway, eds. *Supporting the literacy development of English Learners: Increasing success in all classrooms*. Newark, DE: International Reading Association. 24-40.

Mitchell, V. 1990. *Curriculum and instruction to reduce racial conflict*. (ED322274). New York: ERIC Clearinghouse on Urban Education.

Naiman, N., M. Frolich, H. Stern, and A. Todesco. 1978. *The good language learner*. Toronto: The Modern Language Centre, Ontario Institute for Studies in Education.

National Center on Education and the Economy. 2001. *California Performance Standards*.

National Education Center. 2010. *Provide students with multiple ways to show what they have learned*. Backgrounder. Mar. *www.nea.org*

Neill, M. 2005. Assessment of ELL Students under NCLB: Problems and Solutions. *www.fairtest.org/files/NCLB_assessing_bilingual_students*.

Nieto, S. 1992. We have stories to tell: A case study of Puerto Ricans in children's books. In Harris, V.J., ed. *Teaching multicultural literature in grades K–8*. Norwood, MA: Christopher-Gordon Publishers.

No Child Left Behind Act. Criticisms. Wikipedia. Page last updated on 11 July 2010.

Nunan, D. 1989. *Designing tasks for the communicative classroom*. Cambridge: Cambridge University Press.

O'Malley, J. M., and L. V. Pierce. 1996. *Authentic assessment for English language learners*. New York: Longman.

Ovando, C. J., M. C. Coombs, and V. P. Collier, eds. 2006. *Bilingual and ESL classrooms: Teaching in multicultural contexts*. 4th ed. Boston: McGraw-Hill.

Palacios, I., and J. Arzamendi. 2005. *Second language acquisition*. Spain: Funiber.

Penfield, W., and L. Roberts. 1959. *Speech and brain mechanisms*. New York: Atheneum Press. (reviewed in Ellis, R. 1985).

Peregoy, S. F., and O. F. Boyle. 2008. *Reading, writing, and learning in ESL*. 5th ed. Boston: Pearson.

Prabhu, N. S. 1987. *Second language pedagogy: A perspective*. London: Oxford University Press.

Quiocho, A., and S. H. Ulanoff. 2009. *Differentiated literacy instruction for English language learners*. Boston: Allyn & Bacon.

Reading/Language Arts Framework for California Public Schools. Kindergarten through Grade Twelve. 1999. Sacramento: California Department of Education.

Reid, J. The learning style preferences of ESL students. *TESOL Quarterly*. 21(1): 86-103.

Rennie, J. 1993. ESL and bilingual program models. Eric Digest. *http://www.cal.org/resources/Digest/rennie01.html*

Richards, Platt, and Weber. 1985. Quoted by Ellis, R. The evaluation of communicative tasks. In Tomlinson, B., ed. 1998. *Materials development in language teaching*. Cambridge: Cambridge University Press.

Rinvolucri, M. 1984. *Grammar games: Cognitive, affective and movement activities for ESL students*. Cambridge: Cambridge University Press.

Rinvolucri, M., and P. Davis. 1995. *More grammar games: Cognitive, affective and movement activities for EFL students*. Cambridge: Cambridge University Press.

Rochman, H. 1993. *Against borders: Promoting books for a multicultural world*. Chicago: American Library Association.

Roeder, R. 2009. The effects of phonetic environment on English /æ/ among speakers of Mexican heritage in Michigan. *Toronto Working Papers in Linguistics* (TWPL), Vol. 31.

Rosansky, E. 1975. The critical period for the acquisition of language: Some cognitive developmental considerations. In: *Working Papers on Bilingualism*. 6: 92-102.

Rosenberg, L. 2006. Global Demographic Trends. *Finance and Development*. 43(3) Sep.

Samovar, L. A., and R. E. Porter. 2004. *Communication between cultures*. 5th ed. Thompson and Wadsworth.

Schiffrin, D., D. Tannen, and H. Hamilton, eds. 2003. *The handbook of discourse analysis*. New York: John Wiley & Sons.

Schimel, J. et al. 2000. Running from the shadow: Psychological distancing from others to characteristics people fear in themselves. *Journal of Personality and Social Psychology*. 78(3): 446-62.

Schmidt, R. W. 1990. The role of consciousness in second language acquisition. *Applied Linguistics*. 11(2): 129-58.

Schumm, J. S. 2006. *Reading assessment and instruction for all learners*. New York: The Guilford Press.

Selinker, L. 1972. Interlanguage. *International Review of Applied Linguistics*. vol. 10: 209-231.

Sinclair, J., and M. Coulthard. 1975. *Towards an analysis of discourse*. Oxford: Oxford University Press.

Singer, A., and J.H. Wilson. 2007. *Refugee resettlement in metropolitan America. Migration Policy Institute*. 2010. Washington, D.C. *www.migrationinformation.org*.

Slavin, R. E., and A.Cheung. 2003. *Effective reading programs for English language learners: A best-evidence synthesis*. U.S. Dept. of Education. Institute of Education Sciences.

Snow, C., and M. Hoefnagel-Hohle. 1978. Age differences in second language learning. In: Hatch, ed. *Second language acquisition*. Rowley, MA: Newbury House.

Taylor, O. L. 1990. *Cross-cultural communication: An essential dimension of effective education*. Rev. ed. Chevy Chase, MD: Mid-Atlantic Equity Center.

Teachers of English to Speakers of Other Languages. 1997. *ESL standards for pre-K–12 students*. Alexandria, VA: TESOL.

Teaching Tolerance. n.d. *Anti-gay discrimination in schools*. Southern Poverty Law Center, *http://www.tolerance.org*.

Thomas, W. P., and V. P. Collier. 1995. Language minority student achievement and program effectiveness. Manuscript in preparation. (in Collier, V. P. 1995).

Tollefsen, J. 1991. *Planning language, planning inequality*. New York: Longman.

Tompkins, G. 2009. *Language arts: Patterns of practice*. 7th ed. Upper Saddle River, NJ: Pearson.

Traugott, E. C., and M. L. Pratt. 1980. *Linguistics for students of literature*. San Diego: Harcourt Brace Jovanovich.

2008–2009 Adequate Yearly Progress (AYP) results: Many more schools fail in most states. 2008. National Education Association. *www.nea.org*

United Nations Cyberschoolbus. 1996. *Understanding discrimination*. *www.cyberschoolbus.un.org*, *www.englishclub.com*, *www.wordiq.com*

Unrau, N. 2008. *Content area reading and writing*. 2nd ed. Upper Saddle River, NJ: Pearson.

Ur, P. 1996. *A Course in language teaching*. Cambridge: Cambridge University Press.

Valsiner, J. 2003. Culture and its transfer: Ways of creating general knowledge through the study of cultural particulars. In Lonner, W. J., D. L. Dinnel, S. A. Hayes, and D. N. Sattler, eds. *Online readings in psychology and culture* (Unit 2, Chapter 12), *http://www.wwu.edu/~culture*, Center for Cross-Cultural Research, Western Washington University, Bellingham, WA.

Weir, C. 1993. *Understanding and developing language tests*. Hemel Hempstead: Prentice Hall International.

Widdowson, H. G. 1978. *Teaching language as communication*. Oxford: Oxford University Press.

Willing, K. 1988. Learning strategies as information management: Some definitions for a theory of learning strategies. *Prospect*. 3/2: 139-55.

Yokota, J. 1993. Issues in selecting multicultural children's literature. *Language Arts*. 70: 156-67.

Zainuddin, H. et al. 2007. *Fundamentals of teaching English to speakers of other languages in K–12 mainstream classrooms*. 2nd ed. Dubuque: Kendall/Hunt.

Zwiers, J. 2007. *Building academic language: Essential practices for content classrooms, grades 5–12*. San Francisco: Jossey-Bass.

SAMPLE TEST

SAMPLE TEST

The sample questions that follow illustrate the kinds of questions in the Praxis test. They are not, however, representative of the entire scope of the test either in content or in difficulty.

Listening Section: Oral Grammar And Vocabulary

Directions: In this part of the actual test, you will hear and read a series of short speeches by nonnative speakers of English. Then you will be asked questions about each student's problems in grammar or vocabulary in the recorded speech. You will be allotted ample time to answer the questions.

(Average) (Skill 2.3)

1. Listen to an ESOL student talk about his experience living in the United States.

    (Taped excerpt)

    I'm from Charleston. I live there for four years...

    The verb *live* in the second sentence is incorrect with respect to:

    A. Tense

    B. Gender

    C. Person

    D. Number

(Easy) (Skill 2.3)

2. Listen to an ESOL student talking about her friend's boyfriend.

    (Taped excerpt)

    Your boyfriend is too handsome.

    The adverb *too* is incorrect with regards to:

    A. Usage

    B. Form

    C. Spelling

    D. Word order

(Easy) (Skill 2.3)

3. Listen to an ESOL student talking about an email he received.

    (Taped excerpt)

    Just look at this email from my teacher. He says I was missing my last two tests.

    The verb *was missing* is incorrect with regard to:

    A. Tense

    B. Agreement

    C. Subjunctive

    D. Number

(Average) (Skill 2.3)

4. Listen to an ESOL student talking about her parents.

(Taped excerpt)

My parents deal with much problems every day.

The word *much* is incorrect with regard to the use of _____ nouns.

A. count/no count

B. regular/irregular

C. collective

D. compound

(Rigorous) (Skill 2.3)

5. Listen to an ESOL student talking about love and marriage.

(Taped excerpt)

Many people are afraid of falling in love and to marry.

The words *to marry* are incorrect with regard to:

A. Tense

B. Agreement

C. Parallel structure

D. Adverbial format

(Rigorous) (Skill 2.3)

6. Listen to an ESOL student talking to her friend about English customs.

(Taped excerpt)

One must always be on time.

One refers to:

A. You

B. They

C. The listener

D. The speaker

(Average) (Skill 2.3)

7. Listen to an ESOL student talking about dolphins.

(Taped excerpt)

Dolphins are interesting mammals. They give milk, but it lives in the ocean.

The word *it* is incorrect with respect to:

A. Reference

B. Number

C. Gender

D. Class

(Average) (Skill 2.5)

8. Listen to an ESOL student talking to her friend about life in the United States.

(Taped excerpt)

I think that steak's a little rare.

The word *rare* means:

A. Complicated

B. To be eager

C. Unusual

D. Undercooked

(Easy) (Skill 2.3)

9. Listen to an ESOL student talking about her boss' reorganization of office procedures.

   (Taped excerpt)

   My boss just reorganized our ordering system. As far as I can see, it makes no sense. It has neither rhyme or reason.

   The word *or* in the last sentence is incorrect with regard to:

   A. Parallel structure

   B. Usage

   C. Form

   D. Person

(Easy) (Skill 2.3)

10. Listen to an ESOL student talking about meeting her friend at the airport.

    (Taped excerpt)

    I'll go to pick up Jonathan. She gets in at three.

    The word *she* is incorrect with regard to:

    A. Agreement

    B. Gender

    C. Person

    D. Number

Listening: Pronounciation

Directions: In this part of the actual test, you will hear and read a series of short speeches by nonnative speakers of English. Then you will be asked questions about each student's problems in pronunciation in the recorded speech. You will not be asked to evaluate the student's grammar or vocabulary usage. To help you answer the questions, the speech will be played a second time. You will be allotted ample time to answer the questions.

(Rigorous) (Skill 2.1)

11. Listen to an ESOL student reading the following sentence aloud.

    (Taped excerpt)

    He went on a ship. (Student pronounces *ship* as [shi:p].)

    The error in pronunciation in the word *ship* indicates a problem with:

    A. Diphthongs

    B. Primary cardinal vowels

    C. Triphthongs

    D. Allophones

(Rigorous) (Skill 2.1)

12. Listen to an ESOL student reading the following sentence aloud.

    (Taped excerpt)

    Fish and chips. (Student pronounces *and* as [aend].)

    The error in pronunciation in the word *and* indicates a problem with:

    A. Elision

    B. Assimilation

    C. Phonemes

    D. Weakness

(Rigorous) (Skill 2.1)

13. Listen to an ESOL student reading the following sentence aloud.

    (Taped excerpt)

    Today's Sunday. I am going to church. (Student pronounces church as [shət].)

    The error in pronunciation of the word *church* indicates problems with:

    A. Affricatives

    B. Plosives

    C. Laterals

    D. Glides

(Average) (Skill 2.1)

14. Listen to an ESOL student reading the following sentence aloud.

    (Taped excerpt)

    What a glorious day. Look at that sky. (Student pronounces *sky* as [ski].)

    The error in pronunciation of the word *sky* indicates problems with:

    A. Short vowels

    B. Diphthongs

    C. Triphthongs

    D. Long vowels

(Average) (Skill 2.1)

15. Listen to an ESOL student reading the following sentence aloud.

    (Taped excerpt)

    What are we going to see? (Student pronounces *are* as [är].)

    The error in pronunciation of the word *are* indicates problems with:

    A. Schwa

    B. Stress

    C. Suprasegmentals

    D. Prosody

(Rigorous) (Skill 2.1)

16. Listen to an ESOL student reading the following sentence aloud.

    (Taped excerpt)

    I've three sisters. (Student pronounces *three* as [tri:].)

    The error in pronunciation of the word *three* indicates problems with:

    A. Labials

    B. Affricatives

    C. Palatals

    D. Fricatives

(Rigorous) (Skill 2.1)

17. Listen to an ESOL student reading the following sentence aloud.

    (Taped excerpt)

    Judy read two scripts before giving them to me to study. (Student pronounces *scripts* as [skrIpts].)

    The error in pronunciation of the word *scripts* indicates problems with:

    A. Fricatives

    B. Assimilation

    C. Linking

    D. Elision

(Average) (Skill 2.1)

18. Listen to an ESOL student reading the following sentence aloud.

    (Taped excerpt)

    Susan bought him an elegant watch. (Student pronounces and emphasizes each word.)

    The error in speaking the sentence indicates problems with:

    A. Intonation

    B. Linking sounds

    C. Pitch

    D. Stress-timing

(Average) (Skill 2.1)

19. Listen to an ESOL student reading the following sentence aloud.

    (Taped excerpt)

    Marjorie has lots of problems with her parents. She is such a rebel. (Student pronounces *rebel* as [re/BEL].)

    The error in pronunciation of the word *rebel* indicates problems with:

    A. Pitch

    B. Reduction

    C. Stress

    D. Rhythm

(Rigorous) (Skill 2.1)

20. Listen to an ESOL student reading the following sentence aloud.

    (Taped excerpt)

    What do you like about that movie? (Student pronounces *movie* with a rising voice.)

    The error in pronunciation of the word *movie* indicates problems with:

    A. Pitch

    B. Stress

    C. Function words

    D. Intonation

Foundations of Linguistics and Language Learning

Directions: In this part of the test, you will read a series of short writing samples produced by nonnative speakers of English. You will be asked to identify the errors in the students' writing. Therefore, before taking the test, you should be familiar with the writing of nonnative speakers who are learning English.

Questions 21-23 are based on the following excerpt from an essay describing the student's experience with language learning.

Teachers in my country of foreign languages are well qualified to carry out their duties properly. They must possess a degree from a university language program if they wishes to teach in high school or below. Many also teach in universities, but many need a post-graduate degree. Teachers should be very good at pronouncing the words so their students can imitate him.

(Average) (Skill 2.3)

21. In the first sentence, the error is in the relative order of:

    A. A noun and an adjective

    B. The direct and indirect objects

    C. The subject and object

    D. The prepositional phrases

(Average) (Skill 2.3)

22. The second sentence contains an error in the:

    A. Agreement between the pronoun and verb

    B. Pronoun antecedent and referent

    C. Structure of the subordinate clause

    D. Order of the sentence elements

(Average) (Skill 2.3)

23. The last sentence contains an error in the:

    A. Noun and an adjective

    B. Direct and indirect objects

    C. Subject and the object

    D. Pronoun form

Questions 24–26 are based on an excerpt from an essay describing the student's hometown.

My hometown is Cali, Colombia located in the Cauca River Valley. Cali is surrounded with mountains and cut in half by the Cauca River. Colombians eat many kinds of tropical fruits and vegetables. My favorite dish is a chicken soup with plantains, cassava, potatoes and beef. My mother served this with rice. Visitors can do many exciting things in Cali: riding horses, to swim, and to play tennis.

(Average) (Skill 2.3)

24. In sentence 5, the correct form of the verb *served* should be:

    A. Serves

    B. Serving

    C. Is serving

    D. Has served

(Rigorous) (Skill 2.3)

25. In the sixth sentence, there is an error in the:

    A. Verb tense

    B. Parallel structure

    C. Punctuation

    D. Subject and object

(Rigorous) (Skill 2.3)

26. In the last sentence, the error is in the:

    A. Infinitive

    B. Objective pronoun

    C. Pronoun shift

    D. Subject pronoun

Directions: Each of the questions or statements that follow is followed by four possible answers or completions. Select the one that is best in each of the remaining questions.

(Average) (Skill 2.1)

27. *Bite* and *byte* are examples of which phonographemic differences?

    A. Homonyms

    B. Homographs

    C. Homophones

    D. Heteronyms

(Easy) (Skill 2.1)

28. Words that have the same spelling or pronunciation but different meanings are:

    A. Homonyms

    B. Homographs

    C. Homophones

    D. Heteronyms

(Easy) (Skill 2.1)

29. In the statement "Peter, come here, please," the correct stress would be on:

    A. PEter; PLEASE

    B. peTER; HERE

    C. peTER: COME

    D. peTER; PLEASE

(Easy) (Skill 2.2)

30. If you are studying *morphemic analysis*, then you are studying:

    A. The smallest unit within a language system to which meaning is attached

    B. The root word and the suffix and/or prefix

    C. The way in which speech sounds form patterns

    D. Answers A and B only

(Average) (Skill 2.2)

31. The study of morphemes may provide the student with:

    A. The meaning of the root word

    B. The meaning of the phonemes

    C. Grammatical information

    D. All of the above

(Easy) (Skill 2.3)

32. **If you are studying *syntax*, then you are studying:**

    A. Intonation and accent when conveying a message

    B. The rules for correct sentence structure

    C. The definition of individual words and meanings

    D. The subject-verb-object order of the English sentence

(Easy) (Skill 2.3)

33. **In the following sentence: "Mary had few friends," which word is an example of a countable common noun?**

    A. Mary

    B. had

    C. few

    D. friends

(Average) (Skill 2.3)

34. **To which subcategory of subordinating conjunction does *whether or not* belong?**

    A. Time

    B. Cause and effect

    C. Contrast

    D. Condition

(Average) (Skill 2.3)

35. **The sentence: "The bus was late and he was late, but John still managed to catch it." is an example of a _____ .**

    A. simple sentence

    B. compound sentence

    C. complex sentence

    D. compound-complex sentence

(Easy) (Skill 2.3)

36. **To change the imperative sentence "Come here, Susan" to a polite request, the correct form is:**

    A. "Would you come here, Susan?"

    B. "Do you come here, Susan?"

    C. "Can you come here, Susan?"

    D. "Will you come here, Susan?"

(Average) (Skill 2.4)

37. **Which one of the following is *not* included in the study of semantics?**

    A. Culture

    B. The definition of individual words and meanings

    C. The intonation of the speaker

    D. Meaning that is stored or inherent as well as contextual

(Easy) (Skill 2.4)

38. **A teacher who asks an ELL if he or she has finished the task really means "Finish the assignment." This is an example of:**

    A. Synonyms

    B. Presupposition

    C. Culture in the classroom

    D. Body language

(Easy) (Skill 2.4)

39. **When referring to a wealthy person as a *fat cat*, the speaker is using a/an:**

    A. Cognate

    B. Derivational morpheme

    C. Phrase

    D. Idiom

(Average) (Skill 2.5)

40. **In the English language, all inflections are _____ .**

    A. defined by the noun, i.e., gender and number

    B. suffixes attached to the verb

    C. in the pitch of the voice

    D. in the case

(Easy) (Skill 3.1)

41. **Identify the major factor in the spread of English.**

    A. The invasion of the Germanic tribes in England

    B. The pronunciation changes in Middle English

    C. The extension of the British Empire

    D. The introduction of new words from different cultures

(Easy) (Skill 3.1)

42. **English has grown as a language primarily because of:**

    A. Wars/technology and science

    B. Text messaging/immigrants

    C. Immigrants/technology and science

    D. Contemporary culture/wars

(Easy) (Skill 3.1)

43. **If you are studying *pragmatics*, then you are studying:**

    A. The definition of individual words and meanings

    B. How context impacts the interpretation of language

    C. Meaning that is stored or inherent as well as contextual

    D. All of the above

(Average) (Skill 3.1)

44. **Which one of the following is *not* a factor in people changing their register?**

    A. The relationship between the speakers

    B. The formality of the situation

    C. The attitude towards the listeners and subject

    D. The culture of the speakers

(Rigorous) (Skill 3.2)

45. **In analyzing World Englishes, Kachru classified which of the following countries as members of the outer circle?**

    A. The United Kingdom, Canada, and Australia

    B. Australia, Ireland, and the U.S.

    C. India, Philippines, and Singapore

    D. China, South Korea, and India

(Average) (Skill 3.2)

46. **English as it is spoken by Mississippians is _____.**

    A. the Queen's English

    B. an occupational dialect

    C. a rural dialect

    D. Standard American English

(Average) (Skill 3.3)

47. In 1996, the National Council of Teachers of English and the International Reading Association proposed that:

    A. All ELLs be tested in reading skills

    B. All ELLs be tested in listening and speaking skills

    C. Viewing and visually representing be included in proficiency testing

    D. Testing in the traditional skill areas be continued

(Average) (Skill 4.1)

48. Chomsky's Language Acquisition Device (LAD) includes all of the following hypotheses EXCEPT:

    A. Language learners form hypotheses based on the language they receive

    B. Language learners enter the world as blank slates

    C. Language learners test out hypotheses in speech and texts

    D. Language learners construct language

(Average) (Skill 4.2)

49. A textbook used in an adult education class instructs the students in "How to Buy a Computer" through sample ads and dialogs. Which basic language approach/method is being used in this textbook?

    A. The Silent Way

    B. Notional/functional

    C. Total Physical Response (TPR)

    D. Natural Approach

(Average) (Skill 4.2)

50. By learning phrases such as "According to the author…," ELLs may increase their linguistic abilities. What name has been given to this type of phrase?

    A. Idioms

    B. Utterances

    C. Lexical chunks

    D. Private speech

(Rigorous) (Skill 4.2)

51. Which researcher is most associated with problem-solving activities for language learning?

    A. Gattegno

    B. Prabhu

    C. Wilkins

    D. Lewis

(Easy) (Skill 4.2)

52. L1 and L2 learners follow approximately the same order in learning a language. Identify the correct sequence from the options below.

    A. Silent period, experimental speech, private speech, lexical chunks, formulaic speech

    B. Silent period, private speech, lexical chunks, formulaic speech, experimental speech

    C. Private speech, lexical chunks, silent period, formulaic speech, experimental speech

    D. Private speech, silent period, lexical chunks, formulaic speech, experimental speech

(Average) (Skill 4.2)

53. **Language learners seem to acquire syntax:**

    A. At the same rate in L1 and L2

    B. Faster in L2 than L1

    C. In the same order regardless of whether it is in L1 or L2

    D. In different order for L1

(Rigorous) (Skill 4.2)

54. **"Maria is a profesora" is an example of:**

    A. Dialect

    B. Inter-language

    C. Code-switching

    D. Formulaic speech

(Easy) (Skill 4.3)

55. **Interlanguage is best described as:**

    A. A language characterized by overgeneralization

    B. Bilingualism

    C. A language-learning strategy

    D. A strategy characterized by poor grammar

(Easy) (Skill 4.3)

56. **"The teacher *writted* on the whiteboard" is an example of:**

    A. Simplification

    B. Fossilization

    C. Inter-language

    D. Overgeneralization

(Easy) (Skill 4.3)

57. **Simplification means:**

    A. Adding /ed/ to irregular verbs as a way to use the past tense

    B. Substituting "I have a house beautiful in Miami" for "I have a beautiful house in Miami"

    C. Latinos pronouncing words like *student* as *estudent*

    D. Asking someone, "You like?" instead of, "Do you like this one?"

(Easy) (Skill 4.3)

58. **Which of the following methods of dealing with fossilization is NOT appropriate?**

    A. Ignore mistakes that do not interfere with meaning

    B. Work on items such as the ending /s/ for third person singular in written work

    C. Teacher (or aide) corrects all the errors in the students' writing

    D. Dictating correct sentences of patterns frequently used incorrectly by ELLs

(Average) (Skill 4.3)

59. **Arrange the following sentences, written by ELLs, to show the order of acquisition of negation, ranging from least to most.**

    Sentence 1: Kim didn't went to school.

    Sentence 2: No school. No like.

    Sentence 3: Kim doesn't like to go to school.

    A. Sentence 1, Sentence 2, Sentence 3

    B. Sentence 3, Sentence 2, Sentence 1

    C. Sentence 1, Sentence 3, Sentence 2

    D. Sentence 2, Sentence 1, Sentence 3

(Rigorous) (Skill 4.4)

60. What type of motivation is demonstrated in the following example?

    Marcel arrived in the United States after finishing high school in Belgium. He is highly motivated to improve his English because he has always wanted to work as a translator in the United Nations. He longs for permanent residency in the U.S. to pursue his dream.

    A. Instrumental, intrinsic, state

    B. Integrative, intrinsic, state

    C. Integrative, extrinsic, state

    D. Instrumental, extrinsic, trait

(Average) (Skill 4.5)

61. According to Krashen and Terrell's Input Hypothesis, language learners are able to understand:

    A. Slightly more than they can produce

    B. The same as they speak

    C. Less than they speak

    D. Lots more than they speak

Average) (Skill 4.5)

62. If the teacher circulates around the room answering questions and asking others, which level(s) of scaffolding is she demonstrating?

    A. Modeling

    B. Interactive

    C. Guided

    D. Independent

(Easy) (Skill 5.1)

63. Learning phonics has many advantages. What is one disadvantage of phonics?

    A. Tools are given for decoding written words

    B. Auditory learners learn well with this method

    C. Rules have many exceptions

    D. The sound-symbol connection usually helps with spelling

(Rigorous) (Skill 5.2)

64. Though there are exceptions, the most commonly used method to develop a descriptive text is:

    A. Spatial order

    B. Order of importance

    C. Chronological order

    D. Logical order

(Average) (Skill 5.3)

65. In a bottom-up strategy of literacy development, which one of the following undesirable strategies might a reader use?

    A. Make guesses about what is going to happen

    B. Read all texts at the same speed

    C. Anticipate the contents of the text

    D. Infer meaning from sentences and paragraphs

(Rigorous) (Skill 5.4)

66. Which one of the following developmental skills belongs to the orthographic phase of the alphabetic principle?

    A. Equates the length of a word with its meaning

    B. Confuses similar words

    C. Can sound out regular one-syllable words

    D. Notices familiar parts first, then decodes the unfamiliar parts

(Average) (Skill 5.5)

67. The most appropriate ESOL strategy for readers who do not read in their L1 is to:

    A. Postpone reading until the ELLs acquire intermediate oral language proficiency

    B. Teach cognates and high-frequency words

    C. Develop literacy in L1 first

    D. Use pull-out reading support in L2

(Rigorous) (Skill 5.5)

68. Which of the following options is considered to be a disadvantage of continuing language L1 development in pre-literate children?

    A. Children will not learn English as quickly if they continue to use their native language

    B. Many literary skills from L1 transfer to L2

    C. More mature cognitive development is achieved

    D. Teachers are able to build on previous knowledge

Planning, Implementing, and Managing Instruction

(Average) (Skill 6.1)

69. Advanced TPR might include:

    A. Rapid-fire commands

    B. More advanced vocabulary

    C. Funny commands

    D. All of the above

(Rigorous) (Skill 6.1)

70. Which of the following is NOT a step in the Language Experience Approach?

    A. Students draw a picture to represent something personal about an experience

    B. Students dictate their story to the teacher

    C. The teacher reads the story, revising where necessary

    D. The story is read in later days as a follow-up activity

(Easy) (Skill 6.2)

71. In schools with large immigrant populations of diverse origins, the most commonly used model is:

    A. Submersion

    B. Pull-out

    C. SDAIE

    D. Transition

(Rigorous) (Skill 6.2)

72. Widdowson's definition of *use* and *usage* is well demonstrated in which of the following models?

    A. Canadian French Immersion and Miami-Dade Count models

    B. Submersion with primary language support

    C. Content-based ESL and indigenous language immersion

    D. Communication-based ESL and Grammar-based ESL

(Average) (Skill 7.2)

73. In teaching adults, which of the following is a valid reason for using games?

    A. To relieve tension

    B. To lighten up a heavy lesson

    C. To allow students to learn in a different mode

    D. All of the above

(Average) (Skill 7.3)

74. Which of the following reasons is an advantage of using machines in the ESOL classroom?

    A. They are inexpensive

    B. They are nonjudgmental

    C. They are fun

    D. They are better than teachers

(Rigorous) (Skill 7.4)

75. Which one of the following teaching practices has a positive effect on student writing?

    A. Correction of spelling mistakes

    B. Use of good reading texts

    C. Extensive writing practice

    D. Correction of grammar mistakes

(Average) (Skill 7.5)

76. Why would the average German- or French-speaking ELL need extra work on the English vowels?

    A. English vowels are different from L1 of German and French speakers

    B. There is no sound-symbol correspondence in the English vowels

    C. The sound-symbol connection is consistent in both German and French

    D. English has multiple vowel sounds

(Rigorous) (Skill 7.6)

77. Which one of the following is a strategy used in content-based learning?

    A. Teaching phonics for spelling tests

    B. Teaching grammar points discretely

    C. Providing comprehensible feedback

    D. Using activities for fun only

(Average) (Skill 7.7)

78. Angela needs help in English. Her teacher suggested several things Angela can do to improve her learning strategies. Which of the following is NOT a socioaffective learning strategy?

   A. Read a funny book

   B. Work cooperatively with her classmates

   C. Ask the teacher to speak more slowly

   D. Skim for information

(Rigorous) (Skill 7.8)

79. The Schema Theory of Carrell & Eisterhold suggests that for learning to take place, teachers must:

   A. Integrate content areas with ESOL techniques

   B. Emphasize all four language skills

   C. Present comprehensible input in a meaningful context

   D. Relate new materials to previous knowledge

(Average) (Skill 7.8)

80. Incorporating prior knowledge into L2 learning does NOT:

   A. Permit readers to learn and remember more

   B. Create poor readers

   C. Help readers to evaluate new arguments

   D. Improve comprehension

(Average) (Skill 7.9)

81. Instruction to promote fluency includes:

   A. Developing writing and reading skills separately

   B. Explicit study of vocabulary lists

   C. Role play, phonics instruction, and journal writing

   D. Learning only the specific language for the task at hand

(Average) (Skill 8.2)

82. When planning instruction, Ms. Jones provides her students with various materials on the same subject. Which of the following statements is a valid reason for doing so?

   A. It's easier than summarizing all the material

   B. Children like looking at pictures, and some of the textbooks have few pictures

   C. I believe they should have to work to fill in their Know-Want-Learn charts

   D. No two people learn alike, so I try to provide different materials so everyone has something they like

(Average) (Skill 8.3)

83. Realia often are used in classrooms. Which one of the following would be a valid example of realia for teaching fractions?

   A. A computer

   B. A balance scale

   C. A white mouse

   D. A pizza

(Rigorous) (Skill 9.1)

84. Young children are often considered better language learners than older children or adults, but older children or adults may be able to progress more rapidly in reading instruction because:

    A. They have more worldly experience to help them understand the texts

    B. Their vocabulary concepts in L2 are less developed

    C. They have more language-learning experience

    D. Phonics is the same in L1 and L2

(Rigorous) (Skill 9.1)

85. Abigail is an enthusiastic child who spontaneously cries when watching movies. She challenges the teacher in class but is content to let her classmates make decisions. Which of these learning styles most accurately describes her?

    A. Analytic

    B. Authority-oriented

    C. Communicative

    D. Concrete

(Rigorous) (Skill 9.1)

86. Which of the following should be done prior to initiating a formal referral process for an ELL with possible learning disabilities?

    A. A vision and hearing test

    B. A language diagnostic test

    C. Documentation of at least one intervention

    D. Consultation with the principal about the ELL's progress

(Rigorous) (Skill 9.1)

87. A fifth grader has completed one year in the ESOL program but does not seem to be making progress. Which of the following might indicate a learning disability?

    A. Frequent code switches

    B. Needing extra time to answer questions

    C. Ability to decode successfully but difficulty in comprehension

    D. Dropping of the final consonants of words

(Rigorous) (Skill 11.2)

88. An ELL suspected of having learning difficulties:

    A. May present behavioral problems when asked to produce written work

    B. May demonstrate the ability to learn quickly

    C. Should be analyzed for up to ten weeks using ESOL techniques

    D. May demonstrate the ability to solve problems not dependent on English

(Rigorous) (Skill 9.1)

89. An ELL student may pronounce /free/ instead of /three/. This is an example of:

    A. Omission

    B. Substitution

    C. Distortion

    D. Addition

(Average) (Skill 9.2)

90. Which one of the following policies on classroom management should NOT be established in the classroom by a good classroom manager?

    A. A set of rules

    B. Private talks with different students

    C. Cooperative work groups

    D. Ability groups for regular daily tasks

(Easy) (Skill 9.3)

91. When the teacher is correcting a student's language, the teacher should:

    A. Carefully correct all mistakes

    B. Consider the context of the error

    C. Confirm the error by repeating it

    D. Repeat the student's message but correct it

(Rigorous) (Skill 9.3)

92. Research shows that error correction for ELLs is a delicate business. Which of the following contributes to learning?

    A. Correcting semantic errors

    B. Correcting grammatical errors

    C. Correcting pronunciation

    D. Correcting all written work errors

(Rigorous) (Skill 9.4)

93. The content teacher is trying to establish a text-rich classroom, including some bilingual material. Why is this important to all students?

    A. It emphasizes the importance of reading

    B. It is motivational

    C. It is welcoming

    D. All of the above

(Rigorous) (Skill 9.5)

94. Which of the following activities is the most effective in learning to use the dictionary effectively?

    A. Locating synonyms, phrases, and etymology of words

    B. Looking up definitions and writing a sentence with the words

    C. Rewriting the definition in your own words

    D. Writing down the pronunciation guide and the definition

Assessment

(Rigorous) (Skill 10.1)

95. Which of the following tests is NOT a state-mandated test or a reading/language arts basic skill test?

    A. DRA

    B. WIDA

    C. Iowa Test of Basic Skills

    D. TOEIC

(Rigorous) (Skill 10.2)

96. **What is the main purpose of Title I?**

    A. To test the English level of ELLs

    B. To establish guidelines for the classification of ELLs entering new schools

    C. To establish guidelines for the AYP report

    D. To provide funds to states to support programs for students who need help in math and reading

(Rigorous) (Skill 10.4)

97. **Which one of the following is NOT an authentic way to confirm standardized placement testing results?**

    A. Diagnostic tests

    B. Teacher observations

    C. Previous school records

    D. Oral interviews

(Average) (Skill 10.6)

98. **Which of the following is NOT an acceptable alternative assessment strategy for ELLs?**

    A. Portfolios

    B. Observation

    C. Self-assessment

    D. Essay writing

(Average) (Skill 11.1)

99. **Which of the following accommodations may be allowed for ELLs during assessment?**

    A. Having a translator explain difficult words

    B. Asking proctor to explain certain words or test items

    C. Paraphrasing the prompt

    D. Allowing the use of an English-heritage language translating dictionary

(Rigorous) (Skill 11.2)

100. **Which of the following is NOT an acceptable teaching practice when preparing exceptional students to take tests?**

     A. Give practice timed tests

     B. Use cloze tests

     C. Provide students with study guides

     D. Have the students write practice essays

(Average) (Skill 11.2)

101. **Which of the following is a possible sign of a gifted ELL student?**

     A. Normal development according to parental interview

     B. Speech delayed in L2

     C. Seems to solve logic problems with difficulty

     D. High academic performance in L1

(Rigorous) (Skill 11.3)

102. **Which is the most appropriate method for dealing with a potential cultural bias in tests?**

 A. Translate the tests previous to the actual exam

 B. Provide pictures and graphics during the test

 C. Administer practice tests with time limits

 D. Provide a study guide and give the test orally

(Rigorous) (Skill 11.3)

103. **If a test question asks a student about a Wii video game, which kind of bias may it contain?**

 A. Cultural

 B. Attitudinal

 C. Test/norming

 D. Translation

(Rigorous) (Skill 11.4)

104. **When ELLs are asked to fill in the blanks/gaps on a multiple-choice test, which type of test are they being given?**

 A. First generation

 B. Second generation

 C. Third generation

 D. Traditional

(Rigorous) (Skill 12.1)

105. **Which of the following is a feature of differentiated instruction?**

 A. The teacher plans what all students will learn

 B. The students are placed in learning levels

 C. The gifted student is given a list of learning objectives

 D. Materials are grouped according to ability levels

Cultural and Professional Aspects of the Job

(Average) (Skill 13.1)

106. **Culture and cultural differences:**

 A. Must be addressed by the teacher in the ELL classroom by pointing out cultural similarities and differences

 B. Should be the starting point for learning about how culture affects the ELL's attitude towards education

 C. Positively affects how well ELLs perform in the language classroom

 D. May have a strong emotional influence on the ELL learner

(Rigorous) (Skill 13.3)

107. **ESOL instruction frequently requires the teacher to change her instruction methods. One of the most difficult may be the:**

 A. Wait time

 B. Establishment of group work

 C. Show-and-tell based on different cultures

 D. Extensive reading time

(Rigorous) (Skill 13.3)

108. When Mr. Smith planned his class on plants, he brought in plants and a series of lectures using PowerPoint. His class most likely contains many learners of which of the following types?

    A. Tactile

    B. Auditory

    C. Kinesthetic

    D. Visual

(Rigorous) (Skill 13.7)

109. Which of the following suggestions would the culturally aware teacher disregard, if necessary?

    A. The use of English only in the classroom

    B. Creating a "safe haven" for refugees and at-risk students

    C. Free discussions with women from Muslim cultures

    D. Shaking hands with all parents

(Average) (Skill 13.8)

110. Social factors influence second-language learning because:

    A. Age determines how much one learns

    B. Gender roles are predetermined

    C. Social status is important to the ELL's ability to perform well in the learning situation

    D. Many ELLs cannot ignore their social conditions

(Rigorous) (Skill 14.1)

111. In *Lau v. Nichols* (1974), the Supreme Court ruled that:

    A. School districts may not continue education programs that fail to produce positive results for ELLs

    B. Sexual harassment is prohibited in any school activity on or off campus

    C. Students were denied an "equal" education

    D. Discrimination against students and employers based on race, ethnicity, national origins, disability, or marital status is prohibited

(Rigorous) (Skill 14.2)

112. Which of the following is NOT appropriate when setting high standards for ELLs?

    A. The use of cooperative learning strategies between teacher and students

    B. Establishing goals to accommodate all ELLs

    C. Challenging students cognitively

    D. Developing language and literacy through all instructional activities

(Rigorous) (Skill 14.3)

113. The No Child Left Behind Act established that:

    A. Title I funds are available only if the schools participate in National Assessment of Education Progress

    B. Bilingual programs must be effective and follow three criteria established by a federal court in 1981

    C. High-performing children cannot be used to average out low-performing ELLs

    D. Schools must form and convene assessment committees

(Rigorous) (Skill 14.3)

114. The No Child Left Behind Act requires schools to:

   A. Give assessment in English if the LEP has received 3 years of schooling in the U.S. (except for Puerto Rico)

   B. Measure school districts by status

   C. Inform parents of the school's evaluation

   D. Include LEPs in all academic assessments

(Average) (Skills 7.1, 15.1)

115. What is the teacher's most important role in student-centered learning?

   A. Mentor

   B. Facilitator

   C. Guide

   D. Model

(Rigorous) (Skill 15.3)

116. The affective filter affects how students acquire a second language because:

   A. Learning a second language may make the learner feel vulnerable

   B. The attitude of peers and family is motivating

   C. Motivation is a powerful personal factor

   D. Facilitative anxiety determines our reaction to competition and is positive

(Rigorous) (Skill 15.3)

117. Which of the following personality traits is a "facilitative" anxiety?

   A. Inability to speak before peers

   B. Discrimination

   C. Completes tasks on time

   D. Fear of classmates ridicule

(Rigorous) (Skill 15.5)

118. Transitioning from one class to another or one school to another is challenging for most students. Which of the following activities would NOT make the process easier for most students?

   A. Visiting the new classroom/school

   B. Holding a parental orientation session

   C. Holding a Q&A session with students from the new school

   D. Conducting a Q&A session with the present teachers

(Average) (Skill 15.9)

119. When communicating with parents or caregivers about a student's progress, the teacher should:

   A. Establish grading policies for each assignment

   B. Send notes home well in advance of field trips

   C. Develop rubrics, send them home, and have parents sign and return them

   D. Send notes home about school events when the new term begins

(Rigorous) (Skill 16.2)

120. Which of the following sources would be the most appropriate when inquiring about cultural issues concerning ELLs?

  A. *http://www2.ed.gov/about/offices/list/ies/index.html?src=oc*

  B. *http://www.ed.gov/offices/OCR*

  C. *http://www.cal.org*

  D. *http://www.nabe.org*

Answer Key

ANSWER KEY							
1. A	16. D	31. C	46. C	61. A	76. D	91. D	106. D
2. A	17. D	32. B	47. C	62. B	77. C	92. A	107. A
3. A	18. B	33. D	48. B	63. C	78. D	93. D	108. D
4. A	19. C	34. D	49. B	64. A	79. D	94. A	109. A
5. C	20. D	35. D	50. C	65. B	80. B	95. D	110. D
6. A	21. D	36. A	51. B	66. D	81. C	96. D	111. C
7. B	22. A	37. A	52. B	67. C	82. D	97. A	112. B
8. D	23. D	38. B	53. C	68. A	83. D	98. D	113. C
9. C	24. A	39. D	54. C	69. D	84. A	99. D	114. A
10. B	25. B	40. B	55. C	70. C	85. D	100. D	115. B
11. B	26. C	41. C	56. D	71. B	86. A	101. D	116. A
12. A	27. C	42. C	57. D	72. D	87. C	102. C	117. C
13. A	28. B	43. B	58. C	73. D	88. C	103. A	118. D
14. B	29. A	44. D	59. D	74. B	89. C	104. A	119. C
15. A	30. D	45. C	60. D	75. B	90. D	105. A	120. A

Rigor Table

RIGOR TABLE	
Rigor level	**Questions**
Easy 19%	2, 3, 9, 10, 28, 29, 30, 32, 33, 36, 38, 39, 41, 42, 43, 52, 55, 56, 57, 58, 63, 71, 91
Average Rigor 39%	1, 4, 7, 8, 14, 15, 18, 19, 21, 22, 23, 24, 27, 31, 34, 35, 37, 40, 44, 46, 47, 48, 49, 50, 53, 59, 61, 62, 65, 67, 69, 73, 74, 76, 78, 80, 81, 82, 83, 90, 98, 99, 101, 106, 110, 115, 119
Rigorous 42%	5, 6, 11, 12, 13, 16, 17, 20, 25, 26, 45, 51, 54, 60, 64, 66, 68, 70, 72, 75, 77, 79, 84, 85, 86, 87, 88, 89, 92, 93, 94, 95, 96, 97, 100, 102, 103, 104, 105, 107, 108, 109, 111, 112, 113, 114, 116, 117, 118, 120

Sample Test with Rationales

The sample questions that follow illustrate the kinds of questions in the Praxis test. They are not, however, representative of the entire scope of the test either in content or in difficulty.

Listening Section: Oral Grammar And Vocabulary

Directions: In this part of the actual test, you will hear and read a series of short speeches by nonnative speakers of English. Then you will be asked questions about each student's problems in grammar or vocabulary in the recorded speech. You will be allotted ample time to answer the questions.

(Average) (Skill 2.3)

1. Listen to an ESOL student talk about his experience living in the United States.

   (Taped excerpt)

   I'm from Charleston. I live there for four years…

   The verb *live* in the second sentence is incorrect with respect to:

   A. Tense

   B. Gender

   C. Person

   D. Number

Answer: A. Tense

The pronoun *I* is not gender specific, so it may be used for both male and female people. *I live* for first person singular is correct in both person and number. However, when discussing permanent situations, the present perfect tense *have lived* is the correct tense. Thus, option A is the correct answer.

(Easy) (Skill 2.3)

2. Listen to an ESOL student talking about her friend's boyfriend.

   (Taped excerpt)

   Your boyfriend is too handsome.

   The adverb *too* is incorrect with regards to:

   A. Usage

   B. Form

   C. Spelling

   D. Word order

Answer: A. Usage

The form, spelling, and word order are all correct. Therefore, option A must be the incorrect aspect. The correct word, in this case, would be the adverb *very*.

(Easy) (Skill 2.3)

3. Listen to an ESOL student talking about an email he received.

(Taped excerpt)

Just look at this email from my teacher. He says I was missing my last two tests.

The verb *was missing* is incorrect with regard to:

A. Tense

B. Agreement

C. Subjunctive

D. Number

Answer: A. Tense

In this case, *was missing* is correct with regards to agreement and number. The subjunctive is not indicated. The correct answer is A. The simple past, *missed* is used for reported speech when the speaker is reporting an event in the present.

(Average) (Skill 2.3)

4. Listen to an ESOL student talking about her parents.

(Taped excerpt)

My parents deal with much problems every day.

The word *much* is incorrect with regard to the use of _____ nouns.

A. count/no count

B. regular/irregular

C. collective

D. compound

Answer: A. count/no count

Regular/irregular adjectives such as *good/the best* are irrelevant to the word *much*. *Much* is an adjective, not a collective or compound noun. *Much* is used with uncountable nouns. Therefore, A count/no count nouns is the correct option. *Many*, which is used with plural, countable nouns, would be the correct word.

(Rigorous) (Skill 2.3)

5. Listen to an ESOL student talking about love and marriage.

(Taped excerpt)

Many people are afraid of falling in love and to marry.

The words *to marry* are incorrect with regard to:

A. Tense

B. Agreement

C. Parallel structure

D. Adverbial format

Answer: C. Parallel structure

Gerunds have neither tense nor agreement elements. A gerund is a verb form used as a noun, not an adverb. Thus, option C is the correct one. Since the sentence contains both a gerund and an infinitive, one should be changed so both elements have the same structure. The question is phrased so that *to marry* should be changed to *marrying*.

(Rigorous) (Skill 2.3)

6. **Listen to an ESOL student talking to her friend about English customs.**

   (Taped excerpt)

   One must always be on time.

   One **refers to:**

   A. You

   B. They

   C. The listener

   D. The speaker

   Answer: A. You

   In this question, *one* refers to a general *you*. American English generally uses *you* instead of *one*; both, however, are correct. The correct option is A.

(Average) (Skill 2.3)

7. **Listen to an ESOL student talking about dolphins.**

   (Taped excerpt)

   Dolphins are interesting mammals. They give milk, but it lives in the ocean.

   The word *it* **is incorrect with respect to:**

   A. Reference

   B. Number

   C. Gender

   D. Class

Answer: B. Number

Gender and class refer to the type of pronoun chosen to be used in oral speech or a written text. *Dolphins* is the *referent*. The word *it* is a pronoun that should refer back to its antecedent, *dolphins*. The antecedent *dolphins* is a countable, plural noun indicating that any pronoun referring back to it should also be plural. Answer B is the correct option for the statement because *it* does not agree in number with its antecedent.

(Average) (Skill 2.5)

8. **Listen to an ESOL student talking to her friend about life in the United States.**

   (Taped excerpt)

   I think that steak's a little rare.

   The word *rare* **means:**

   A. Complicated

   B. To be eager

   C. Unusual

   D. Undercooked

Answer: D. Undercooked

Complicated means *involved, intricate* and is incorrect. B, C, and D are all definitions of different forms of the word *rare*. Definition B is used in the present participle, while C and D are adjectives. Answer D is the correct response because in the context of referring to food, *rare* means *undercooked, partially raw*.

(Easy) (Skill 2.3)

9. Listen to an ESOL student talking about her boss' reorganization of office procedures.

(Taped excerpt)

My boss just reorganized our ordering system. As far as I can see, it makes no sense. It has neither rhyme or reason.

The word *or* in the last sentence is incorrect with regard to:

A. Parallel structure

B. Usage

C. Form

D. Person

Answer: C. Form

Parallel structure, usage, and person do not apply in this case since *neither/nor* is a correlative conjunction. With the negative *neither*, the correct form is *nor*. *Or* is used with the positive *either*. The correct answer is C.

(Easy) (Skill 2.3)

10. Listen to an ESOL student talking about meeting her friend at the airport.

(Taped excerpt)

I'll go to pick up Jonathan. She gets in at three.

The word *she* is incorrect with regard to:

A. Agreement

B. Gender

C. Person

D. Number

Answer: B. Gender

The third person singular of the verb *get* is *gets*, so the agreement of number and person are correct. The incorrect gender has been used because Jonathan is a male name. Thus, *he* would be the correct pronoun. Option B is the best selection.

Listening: Pronounciation

Directions: In this part of the actual test, you will hear and read a series of short speeches by nonnative speakers of English. Then you will be asked questions about each student's problems in pronunciation in the recorded speech. You will not be asked to evaluate the student's grammar or vocabulary usage. To help you answer the questions, the speech will be played a second time. You will be allotted ample time to answer the questions.

(Rigorous) (Skill 2.1)

11. Listen to an ESOL student reading the following sentence aloud.

(Taped excerpt)

He went on a ship. (Student pronounces *ship* as [shi:p].)

The error in pronunciation in the word *ship* indicates a problem with:

A. Diphthongs

B. Primary cardinal vowels

C. Triphthongs

D. Allophones

Answer: B. Primary cardinal vowels

Diphthongs are combinations of two phonemes that glide together. Triphthongs are vowel sounds in which three vowels are sounded in a sequence, such as *fire* or *flower*. Allophones are sounds regional speakers make. Thus, answer B is the best option since the pronunciation of the vowel /i/ is in question.

(Rigorous) (Skill 2.1)

12. **Listen to an ESOL student reading the following sentence aloud.**

    (Taped excerpt)

    Fish and chips. (Student pronounces *and* as [aend].)

    The error in pronunciation in the word *and* indicates a problem with:

    A. Elision

    B. Assimilation

    C. Phonemes

    D. Weakness

Answer: A. Elision

Assimilation is when a phoneme is spoken differently when it is near another phoneme. This is more common in rapid, casual speech. Weakness in English is defined as reduction, assimilation, and elision. The question refers to a specific type of weakness—elision—where two phonemes disappear to create an /n/ in typical speech. The best option is A.

(Rigorous) (Skill 2.1)

13. **Listen to an ESOL student reading the following sentence aloud.**

    (Taped excerpt)

    Today's Sunday. I am going to church. (Student pronounces church as [shət].)

    The error in pronunciation of the word *church* indicates problems with:

    A. Affricatives

    B. Plosives

    C. Laterals

    D. Glides

Answer: A. Affricatives

English has six plosive consonants. The only consonant classified as a lateral alveolar in English is the /l/. Glides refer to diphthongs where sound does not remain consonant but glides from one sound to another. Affricatives are stop consonants that are released slowly into a period of fricative noise such as the /ch/ in church. The correct option is A.

(Average) (Skill 2.1)

14. **Listen to an ESOL student reading the following sentence aloud.**

    (Taped excerpt)

    What a glorious day. Look at that sky. (Student pronounces *sky* as [ski].)

    The error in pronunciation of the word *sky* indicates problems with:

    A. Short vowels

    B. Diphthongs

    C. Triphthongs

    D. Long vowels

Answer: B. Diphthongs

Short vowels are those in such words as *pat, pet, pit, pot,* and *put.* Long vowels are those such as *take, mete, mike, toke,* and *mute.* Triphthongs are vowel sounds in which three vowels are sounded in a sequence, such as *fire* or *flower.* The diphthong [skaI] should be used instead of the pure long vowel /i/. Therefore, B is the correct choice.

(Average) (Skill 2.1)

15. **Listen to an ESOL student reading the following sentence aloud.**

    (Taped excerpt)

    What are we going to see? (Student pronounces *are* as [är].)

    The error in pronunciation of the word *are* indicates problems with:

    A. Schwa

    B. Stress

    C. Suprasegmentals

    D. Prosody

Answer: A. Schwa

The speaker does not have problems with stress at the word or sentence level. Suprasegmentals refer to teaching the "big picture," or the characteristics that extend over entire utterances versus individual elements, such as how to pronounce the letter /d/. Stress is an element of prosody; the other element is intonation. The schwa /ə/ is used as a symbol to represent an "emptiness" in pronunciation. For example, the /er/ at the end of many words is pronounced using the schwa. The correct answer is A.

(Rigorous) (Skill 2.1)

16. **Listen to an ESOL student reading the following sentence aloud.**

    (Taped excerpt)

    I've three sisters. (Student pronounces *three* as [tri:].)

    The error in pronunciation of the word *three* indicates problems with:

    A. Labials

    B. Affricatives

    C. Palatals

    D. Fricatives

Answer: D. Fricatives

Labials refer to a group of consonants in which the lips form their distinctive sound. The palatals are those sounds made by raising the front of the tongue towards the hard palate. Affricatives are stop consonants that are released slowly into a period of fricative noise, such as the /ch/ in *church.* The /th/ sound in English is represented as a dental fricative and may be voiced or voiceless. The /th/ sound in *three* is voiced and represented by the /θ/.

(Rigorous) (Skill 2.1)

17. Listen to an ESOL student reading the following sentence aloud.

    (Taped excerpt)

    Judy read two scripts before giving them to me to study. (Student pronounces *scripts* as [skrɪpts].)

    The error in pronunciation of the word *scripts* indicates problems with:

    A. Fricatives

    B. Assimilation

    C. Linking

    D. Elision

    Answer: D. Elision

    Assimilation is when a phoneme is spoken differently when it is near another phoneme. This is more common in rapid, casual speech. Linking refers to sounds that join with the following sounds to produce a linked sound, such as *Alice in Wonderland*, where the /c/ becomes an /s/ and links with *in* to become /sin/. Weakness in English is defined as reduction, assimilation, and elision. The question refers to a specific type of weakness, elision, where three phonemes appear together. The most likely scenario is that native speakers would drop the middle phoneme /t/, pronouncing the word as [skrɪps]. The best option is A.

(Average) (Skill 2.1)

18. Listen to an ESOL student reading the following sentence aloud.

    (Taped excerpt)

    Susan bought him an elegant watch. (Student pronounces and emphasizes each word.)

    The error in speaking the sentence indicates problems with:

    A. Intonation

    B. Linking sounds

    C. Pitch

    D. Stress-timing

    Answer: B. Linking sounds

    Intonation concerns the tone pattern of speech and is produced by changing the vocal pitch. Pitch refers to the rising/falling pattern of the voiced speech. Some linguists refer to English as a stress-timed language, whereas many other languages, for instance, Spanish, are syllable-timed. If a student pronounces and emphasizes each word, then the student has trouble with linking sounds, because *bought him* would surely be linked as /boughim/.

(Average) (Skill 2.1)

19. Listen to an ESOL student reading the following sentence aloud.

    (Taped excerpt)

    Marjorie has lots of problems with her parents. She is such a rebel. (Student pronounces *rebel* as [re/BEL].)

    The error in pronunciation of the word *rebel* indicates problems with:

    A. Pitch

    B. Reduction

    C. Stress

    D. Rhythm

    Answer: C. Stress

    Pitch refers to the high or low tone of the voice. Stress refers to accent. Reduction has to do with the speaker reducing certain phonemes in order to produce simpler, easier-to-pronounce utterances. Rhythm is the sound pattern achieved through stressed and unstressed syllables. The stress, or accent, of certain words in English changes their grammatical function in an utterance. The word [re/BEL] is a verb. The correct word should be [REB/el], a noun. C is the best option.

(Rigorous) (Skill 2.1)

20. Listen to an ESOL student reading the following sentence aloud.

    (Taped excerpt)

    What do you like about that movie? (Student pronounces *movie* with a rising voice.)

    The error in pronunciation of the word *movie* indicates problems with:

    A. Pitch

    B. Stress

    C. Function words

    D. Intonation

    Answer: D. Intonation

    Pitch refers to the high or low tone of the voice. Stress refers to accent. Grammatical or function words are words that show how other words and sentences relate to each other, e.g., *in, the, which,* etc. Intonation concerns the pattern of pitch and stress changes uttered in a phrase or a sentence. The best option is D.

Foundations of Linguistics and Language Learning

Directions: In this part of the test, you will read a series of short writing samples produced by nonnative speakers of English. You will be asked to identify the errors in the students' writing. Therefore, before taking the test, you should be familiar with the writing of nonnative speakers who are learning English.

Questions 21-23 are based on the following excerpt from an essay describing the student's experience with language learning.

Teachers in my country of foreign languages are well qualified to carry out their duties properly. They must possess a degree from a university language program if they wishes to teach in high school or below. Many also teach in universities, but many need a post-graduate degree. Teachers should be very good at pronouncing the words so their students can imitate him.

(Average) (Skill 2.3)

21. In the first sentence, the error is in the relative order of:

   A. A noun and an adjective

   B. The direct and indirect objects

   C. The subject and object

   D. The prepositional phrases

Answer: D. The prepositional phrases

The error lies in the order of the first two prepositional phrases. The sentence should read *Teachers of foreign languages in my country....* Prepositional phrases are normally placed as close to the words they modify as possible to avoid confusion. Answer D is the correct option.

(Average) (Skill 2.3)

22. The second sentence contains an error in the:

   A. Agreement between the pronoun and verb

   B. Pronoun antecedent and referent

   C. Structure of the subordinate clause

   D. Order of the sentence elements

Answer: A. Agreement between the pronoun and verb

The sentence should read *if they wish to teach in high school or below.* Therefore, the correct option is A.

(Average) (Skill 2.3)

23. The last sentence contains an error in the:

   A. Noun and an adjective

   B. Direct and indirect objects

   C. Subject and the object

   D. Pronoun form

Answer: D. Pronoun form

In the last sentence, the antecedent of *they* is *their students.* Therefore, the objective form should be used in the phrase *so their students can imitate him.* The correct option is D.

Questions 24–26 are based on an excerpt from an essay describing the student's hometown.

My hometown is Cali, Colombia located in the Cauca River Valley. Cali is surrounded with mountains and cut in half by the Cauca River. Colombians eat many kinds of tropical fruits and vegetables. My favorite dish is a chicken soup with plantains, cassava, potatoes and beef. My mother served this with rice. Visitors can do many exciting things in Cali: riding horses, to swim, and to play tennis.

(Average) (Skill 2.3)

24. In sentence 5, the correct form of the verb *served* should be:

   A. Serves

   B. Serving

   C. Is serving

   D. Has served

   Answer: A. Serves

   The author is discussing how his mother serves the chicken soup—always. Therefore, the simple present tense is used. Selection A is the correct option.

(Rigorous) (Skill 2.3)

25. In the sixth sentence, there is an error in the:

   A. Verb tense

   B. Parallel structure

   C. Punctuation

   D. Subject and object

Answer: B. Parallel structure

The items in this series (*riding horses, to swim, and to play tennis*) should all have the same structure. They should all be gerunds or infinitives, not a mix of the two. Thus, answer B is the correct answer.

(Rigorous) (Skill 2.3)

26. In the last sentence, the error is in the:

   A. Infinitive

   B. Objective pronoun

   C. Pronoun shift

   D. Subject pronoun

   Answer: C. Pronoun shift

   The author may confuse his readers if he changes his writing from *his* point of view to that of Colombians in general. He should be careful to use first person throughout his paragraph and not change to *We*. Therefore, C is the correct option.

Directions: Each of the questions or statements that follow is followed by four possible answers or completions. Select the one that is best in each of the remaining questions.

(Average) (Skill 2.1)

27. *Bite* and *byte* are examples of which phonographemic differences?

   A. Homonyms

   B. Homographs

   C. Homophones

   D. Heteronyms

Answer: C. Homophones

Homonyms is a general term for words with two or more meanings. *Homographs* are two or more words with the same spelling or pronunciation but different meanings. *Heteronyms* are two or more words that have the same spelling but different meanings and spellings. *Homophones* are words that have the same pronunciation but different meanings and spellings. C is the correct response.

(Easy) (Skill 2.1)

28. Words that have the same spelling or pronunciation but different meanings are:

    A. Homonyms

    B. Homographs

    C. Homophones

    D. Heteronyms

Answer: B. Homographs

See the explanation for question 27.

(Easy) (Skill 2.1)

29. In the statement "Peter, come here, please," the correct stress would be on:

    A. PEter; PLEASE

    B. peTER; HERE

    C. peTER: COME

    D. peTER; PLEASE

Answer: A. PEter; PLEASE

(Easy) (Skill 2.2)

30. If you are studying *morphemic analysis*, then you are studying:

    A. The smallest unit within a language system to which meaning is attached

    B. The root word and the suffix and/or prefix

    C. The way in which speech sounds form patterns

    D. Answers A and B only

Answer: D. Answers A and B only

The study of the way in which speech sounds form patterns is called phonology. The smallest unit within a language system to which meaning is attached is a morpheme. The root word and the suffix and/or prefix are components of morphemes and basic to the analysis of a word. Therefore, both A and B are necessary for the study of morphemic analysis, so the correct answer is D.

(Average) (Skill 2.2)

31. The study of morphemes may provide the student with:

    A. The meaning of the root word

    B. The meaning of the phonemes

    C. Grammatical information

    D. All of the above

Answer: C. Grammatical information

The meaning of the root word comes from its source or origin, and the meaning of phonemes relates to their sounds. The correct answer is C. Grammatical morphemes give information that shows how the parts of a sentence relate to each other (e.g., prepositions or articles).

(Easy) (Skill 2.3)

32. If you are studying *syntax*, then you are studying:

   A. Intonation and accent when conveying a message

   B. The rules for correct sentence structure

   C. The definition of individual words and meanings

   D. The subject-verb-object order of the English sentence

Answer: B. The rules for correct sentence structure

The intonation and accent used when conveying a message are pitch and stress. The definition of individual words and meanings is semantics. The subject-verb-object order is the correct order for most English sentences, but the rules for correct sentence structure refer to syntax, so B is the best option.

(Easy) (Skill 2.3)

33. In the following sentence: "Mary had few friends," which word is an example of a countable common noun?

   A. Mary

   B. had

   C. few

   D. friends

Answer: D. friends

Option A is incorrect because Mary is a countable *proper* noun. Option B is a verb. Option C is used when referring to countable nouns but is an adjective. Option D is the correct choice because one's friends may be counted.

(Average) (Skill 2.3)

34. To which subcategory of subordinating conjunction does *whether or not* belong?

   A. Time

   B. Cause and effect

   C. Contrast

   D. Condition

Answer: D. Condition

Time conjunctions (Option A) are those referring to time, such as *after, before, while,* etc. Option B, cause and effect conjunctions, includes *because, now that, since,* etc. Option C refers to conjunctions such as *although, even though, though,* etc. Condition conjunctions (Option D) include *if, unless, whether or not,* etc. Option D is the correct choice.

(Average) (Skill 2.3)

35. The sentence: "The bus was late and he was late, but John still managed to catch it." is an example of a _____ .

   A. simple sentence

   B. compound sentence

   C. complex sentence

   D. compound-complex sentence

Answer: D. compound-complex sentence

The sentence includes two independent clauses: *The bus was late and he was late* and *John still managed to catch it.* The first clause is also a compound clause with two independent clauses: *The bus was late* and *he was late.* Thus, our sentence is compound-complex.

(Easy) (Skill 2.3)

36. To change the imperative sentence "Come here, Susan" to a polite request, the correct form is:

    A. "Would you come here, Susan?"

    B. "Do you come here, Susan?"

    C. "Can you come here, Susan?"

    D. "Will you come here, Susan?"

    Answer: A. "Would you come here, Susan?"

    In polite requests with *you* as the subject, *would you* and *will you* have the same meaning. *Would you* is used more often and considered more polite. The degree of politeness, however, is determined by the tone of the speaker's voice.

(Average) (Skill 2.4)

37. Which one of the following is *not* included in the study of semantics?

    A. Culture

    B. The definition of individual words and meanings

    C. The intonation of the speaker

    D. Meaning that is stored or inherent as well as contextual

Answer: A. Culture

Because semantics refers to the definition of individual words and meanings, the intonation of the speaker, and meaning that is stored or inherent as well as contextual, option A is the best response.

(Easy) (Skill 2.4)

38. A teacher who asks an ELL if he or she has finished the task really means "Finish the assignment." This is an example of:

    A. Synonyms

    B. Presupposition

    C. Culture in the classroom

    D. Body language

    Answer: B. Presupposition

    Synonyms are two words that mean the same thing. The statement "Finish the assignment" has no particular significance and the teacher is not using body language when she makes a simple statement. The best option is B, where the teacher is implying that she can see that the assignment has not been finished and is issuing a command to finish it.

(Easy) (Skill 2.4)

39. When referring to a wealthy person as a *fat cat*, the speaker is using a/an:

    A. Cognate

    B. Derivational morpheme

    C. Phrase

    D. Idiom

Answer: D: Idiom

Idioms are new meanings assigned to words that already have a meaning in a language. The expression *fat cat* literally means a cat that is fat. However, it has become an idiomatic way to describe a wealthy person.

(Average) (Skill 2.5)

40. **In the English language, all inflections are _____ .**

A. defined by the noun, i.e., gender and number

B. suffixes attached to the verb

C. in the pitch of the voice

D. in the case

Answer: B. suffixes attached to the verb

In English, the only inflections that occur are suffixes attached to the verb. The correct choice is B.

(Easy) (Skill 3.1)

41. **Identify the major factor in the spread of English.**

A. The invasion of the Germanic tribes in England

B. The pronunciation changes in Middle English

C. The extension of the British Empire

D. The introduction of new words from different cultures

Answer: C. The extension of the British Empire

The sun never set on the British Empire during the 19th century, causing English to spread all over the world. (The pre-dominance of English in databanks—an estimated 80 to 90 percent of the world's databanks are in English—means that English remains the foremost language in the world today.) Thus, option C is correct.

(Easy) (Skill 3.1)

42. **English has grown as a language primarily because of:**

A. Wars/technology and science

B. Text messaging/immigrants

C. Immigrants/technology and science

D. Contemporary culture/wars

Answer: C. Immigration/technology and science

While all of the answer choices have influenced the growth of English, new immigrants continually adding new words to the language is the most influential factor. The second-largest body of new words comes from technology and science, making option C the best option.

(Easy) (Skill 3.1)

43. **If you are studying *pragmatics*, then you are studying:**

    A. The definition of individual words and meanings

    B. How context impacts the interpretation of language

    C. Meaning that is stored or inherent as well as contextual

    D. All of the above

    Answer: B. How context impacts the interpretation of language

    The definition of individual words and meanings refers to semantics. Meaning that is stored or inherent as well as contextual refers to the lexicon of a language. The best option is B because pragmatics is the study of how context impacts the interpretation of language.

(Average) (Skill 3.1)

44. **Which one of the following is NOT a factor in people changing their register?**

    A. The relationship between the speakers

    B. The formality of the situation

    C. The attitude towards the listeners and subject

    D. The culture of the speakers

    Answer: D. The culture of the speakers

    People change their register depending on the relationship between the speakers, the formality of the situation, and the attitude towards the listeners and the subject. Answer D, the culture of the speakers, is not a reason for people to change their register.

(Rigorous) (Skill 3.2)

45. **In analyzing World Englishes, Kachru classified which of the following countries as members of the outer circle?**

    A. The United Kingdom, Canada, and Australia

    B. Australia, Ireland, and the U.S.

    C. India, Philippines, and Singapore

    D. China, South Korea, and India

    Answer: C. India, Philippines, and Singapore

    The outer circle is made up of ex-colonies of the traditional English-speaking countries. In the inner circle are the traditional English-speaking countries such as the United Kingdom, the United States, Ireland, New Zealand, Australia, and Canada. C is the correct answer.

(Average) (Skill 3.2)

46. **English as it is spoken by Mississippians is _____.**

    A. the Queen's English

    B. an occupational dialect

    C. a rural dialect

    D. Standard American English

    Answer: C. a rural dialect

    Options A and D refer to the standard speech of the UK and the U.S. respectively. Option B refers to the idiosyncratic speech of workers such as coal miners or IT techs. Option C is the best choice because it refers to a region of the United States considered to have a southern drawl, which is a regional, rural dialect.

(Average) (Skill 3.3)

47. In 1996, the National Council of Teachers of English and the International Reading Association proposed that:

    A. All ELLs be tested in reading skills

    B. All ELLs be tested in listening and speaking skills

    C. Viewing and visually representing be included in proficiency testing

    D. Testing in the traditional skill areas be continued

Answer: C. Viewing and visually representing be included in proficiency testing

All students are already tested in the four basic skill areas of speaking, listening, reading, and writing. Therefore, options A, B, and D are eliminated. Option C is correct because the recommendation wished to include new areas to reflect the growing importance of visual materials. Thus, option C is the best choice.

(Average) (Skill 4.1)

48. Chomsky's Language Acquisition Device (LAD) includes all of the following hypotheses EXCEPT:

    A. Language learners form hypotheses based on the language they receive

    B. Language learners enter the world as blank slates

    C. Language learners test out hypotheses in speech and texts

    D. Language learners construct language

Answer: B. Language learners enter the world as blank slates

The essence of Chomsky's theory is that children do not enter the world as a blank slate, but rather have an LAD, which permits the construction of their language regardless of which language it may be. The LAD is innate. Therefore, Option B is the correct choice because it does not support Chomsky's theory.

(Average) (Skill 4.2)

49. A textbook used in an adult education class instructs the students in "How to Buy a Computer" through sample ads and dialogs. Which basic language approach/method is being used in this textbook?

    A. The Silent Way

    B. Notional/functional

    C. Total Physical Response (TPR)

    D. Natural Approach

Answer: B. Notional/functional

Option A, the Silent Way, would not instruct students in dialogs but, rather, would expect them to construct their own. Option C, TPR, uses physical movements to follow basic instructions. Option D, the Natural Approach, emphasizes "natural speech," so pre-written dialogs would violate this principle. The Notional (sequence of events) and functional (buying a computer) method would provide adult learners with the concepts they would use in their daily lives. Option B is the best choice.

(Average) (Skill 4.2)

50. By learning phrases such as "According to the author…," ELLs may increase their linguistic abilities. What name has been given to this type of phrase?

    A. Idioms

    B. Utterances

    C. Lexical chunks

    D. Private speech

Answer: C. Lexical chunks

Option A may be discarded because the phrase means what it says and has no metaphoric meaning. Option B may be excluded because context is relatively unimportant and the literal meaning is unaffected by its context. Option D refers to a pre-speaking phase of L2 development. Option C, lexical chunks, proposed by Lewis, suggests that LLs who learn fixed and semi-fixed chunks (blocks) of language that do not change increase their lexis considerably. C is the best choice.

(Rigorous) (Skill 4.2)

51. Which researcher is most associated with problem-solving activities for language learning?

    A. Gattegno

    B. Prabhu

    C. Wilkins

    D. Lewis

Answer: B. Prabhu

Option A, Gattegno, is associated with the Silent Way. Option C, Wilkins, developed the Notional/Functional Syllabus. Option D, Lewis, proposed the idea of lexical chunks. The correct option is B. Prabhu, who developed the idea of "gap" activities, which include reasoning and problem-solving.

(Easy) (Skill 4.2)

52. L1 and L2 learners follow approximately the same order in learning a language. Identify the correct sequence from the options below.

    A. Silent period, experimental speech, private speech, lexical chunks, formulaic speech

    B. Silent period, private speech, lexical chunks, formulaic speech, experimental speech

    C. Private speech, lexical chunks, silent period, formulaic speech, experimental speech

    D. Private speech, silent period, lexical chunks, formulaic speech, experimental speech

Answer: B. Silent period, private speech, lexical chunks, formulaic speech, experimental speech

Research states that ELLs go through a predictable, sequential series of stages in language learning. The correct order is B.

(Average) (Skill 4.2)

53. **Language learners seem to acquire syntax:**

    A. At the same rate in L1 and L2

    B. Faster in L2 than L1

    C. In the same order regardless of whether it is in L1 or L2

    D. In different order for L1

Answer: C. In the same order regardless of whether it is in L1 or L2

All language learners must progress through the same hierarchical steps in their language learning process. They go from the least to the most complicated stages. regardless of whether it is in the L1 or L2.

(Rigorous) (Skill 4.2)

54. **"Maria is a profesora" is an example of:**

    A. Dialect

    B. Inter-language

    C. Code-switching

    D. Formulaic speech

Answer: C. Code-switching

Dialect is any form or variety of a spoken language peculiar to a region, community, social group, etc. Inter-language is the language spoken by ELLs that is between their L1 and L2. Formulaic speech is speech that is ritualistic in nature and perhaps used for social politeness rather than information.

Sociolinguistics is a very broad term used to understand the relationship between language and people, including the phenomenon of people switching languages during a conversation. A person may switch languages when a word is not known in the other language. Option C is the correct option.

(Easy) (Skill 4.3)

55. **Interlanguage is best described as:**

    A. A language characterized by overgeneralization

    B. Bilingualism

    C. A language-learning strategy

    D. A strategy characterized by poor grammar

Answer: C. A language-learning strategy

Interlanguage occurs when the second-language learner lacks proficiency in L2 and tries to compensate for his or her lack of fluency in the new language. Three components are overgeneralization, simplification, and L1 interference, or language transfer. Therefore, answer A is only one component of interlanguage, making option C the correct answer.

(Easy) (Skill 4.3)

56. "The teacher *writted* on the whiteboard" is an example of:

A. Simplification

B. Fossilization

C. Inter-language

D. Overgeneralization

Answer: D. Overgeneralization

In this case, the ELL has tried to apply the rule of /ed/ endings to an irregular verb to form the past tense verb, i.e., he has used overgeneralization to create an incorrect verb form. The correct answer is D.

(Easy) (Skill 4.3)

57. **Simplification means:**

A. Adding /ed/ to irregular verbs as a way to use the past tense

B. Substituting "I have a house beautiful in Miami" for "I have a beautiful house in Miami"

C. Latinos pronouncing words like *student* as *estudent*

D. Asking someone, "You like?" instead of, "Do you like this one?"

Answer: D. Asking someone, "You like?" instead of, "Do you like this one?"

Simplification is a common learner error involving simplifying the language when the correct structures have not been internalized. In this case, the correct question form has not been acquired, though the ELL's meaning is clear.

(Easy) (Skill 4.3)

58. **Which of the following methods of dealing with fossilization is NOT appropriate?**

A. Ignore mistakes that do not interfere with meaning

B. Work on items such as the ending /s/ for third person singular in written work

C. Teacher (or aide) corrects all the errors in the students' writing

D. Dictating correct sentences of patterns frequently used incorrectly by ELLs

Answer: C. Teacher (or aide) corrects all the errors in the students' writing

Peer correction is an effective way of dealing with fossilization. Both the ELL and his or her peer have the opportunity to analyze errors in a nonconfrontational way.

(Average) (Skill 4.3)

59. **Arrange the following sentences, written by ELLs, to show the order of acquisition of negation, ranging from least to most.**

Sentence 1: Kim didn't went to school.

Sentence 2: No school. No like.

Sentence 3: Kim doesn't like to go to school.

A. Sentence 1, Sentence 2, Sentence 3

B. Sentence 3, Sentence 2, Sentence 1

C. Sentence 1, Sentence 3, Sentence 2

D. Sentence 2, Sentence 1, Sentence 3

Answer: D. Sentence 2, Sentence 1, Sentence 3

Sentence 1 demonstrates correct syntax except for the negative irregular verb. Sentence 2 demonstrates simplification, or early speech. Sentence 3 shows mastery of English syntax. The correct order of acquisition of language is D.

(Rigorous) (Skill 4.4)

60. **What type of motivation is demonstrated in the following example?**

   Marcel arrived in the United States after finishing high school in Belgium. He is highly motivated to improve his English because he has always wanted to work as a translator in the United Nations. He longs for permanent residency in the U.S. to pursue his dream.

   A. Instrumental, intrinsic, state

   B. Integrative, intrinsic, state

   C. Integrative, extrinsic, state

   D. Instrumental, extrinsic, trait

Answer: D. Instrumental, extrinsic, trait

Instrumental motivation concerns acquiring language for specific reasons, such as getting a job. Integrative motivation concerns the desire to communicate with another culture. Because Marcel desires a specific job, we can eliminate options B and C. Marcel's job plans are an external motivating factor (extrinsic), so option A, intrinsic (internal motivation) can be eliminated. Because Marcel's plans are long-standing, they may be classified as a trait and not as a state (a temporary condition). Option D is the correct choice.

(Average) (Skill 4.5)

61. **According to Krashen and Terrell's Input Hypothesis, language learners are able to understand:**

   A. Slightly more than they can produce

   B. The same as they speak

   C. Less than they speak

   D. Lots more than they speak

Answer: A. Slightly more than they can produce

Krashen and Terrell's Input Hypothesis ($i + 1$) states that instruction should be at a level slightly above the language learner's production level. In this way, the learner will have the basis with which to understand but will have to figure out the unknown language in context.

(Average) (Skill 4.5)

62. **If the teacher circulates around the room answering questions and asking others, which level(s) of scaffolding is she demonstrating?**

   A. Modeling

   B. Interactive

   C. Guided

   D. Independent

Answer: B. Interactive

If the teacher was modeling, she would be demonstrating correct pronunciation or syntax to the students. If the ELLs were at an independent level, they would not need scaffolding. By circulating and answering questions, she can be interactive and guide the learning—possibly through asking other questions.

(Easy) (Skill 5.1)

63. Learning phonics has many advantages. What is one disadvantage of phonics?

    A. Tools are given for decoding written words

    B. Auditory learners learn well with this method

    C. Rules have many exceptions

    D. The sound-symbol connection usually helps with spelling

    Answer: C. Rules have many exceptions

    Options A, B, and D are all advantages of phonics. Only C is a disadvantage.

(Rigorous) (Skill 5.2)

64. Though there are exceptions, the most commonly used method to develop a descriptive text is:

    A. Spatial order

    B. Order of importance

    C. Chronological order

    D. Logical order

    Answer: A. Spatial order

    Option B, order of importance, is used to develop evaluative text; option C, chronological order, is used to develop narration; and option D, logical order, is used to develop classification texts. Option A, spatial order, is used to develop descriptive texts and is the correct choice.

(Average) (Skill 5.3)

65. In a bottom-up strategy of literacy development, which one of the following undesirable strategies might a reader use?

    A. Make guesses about what is going to happen

    B. Read all texts at the same speed

    C. Anticipate the contents of the text

    D. Infer meaning from sentences and paragraphs

    Answer: B. Read all texts at the same speed

    Options A, C, and D are all advantages of a top-down strategy and are desirable reading strategies. Only option B is undesirable and the correct answer.

(Rigorous) (Skill 5.4)

66. Which one of the following developmental skills belongs to the orthographic phase of the alphabetic principle?

    A. Equates the length of a word with its meaning

    B. Confuses similar words

    C. Can sound out regular one-syllable words

    D. Notices familiar parts first, then decodes the unfamiliar parts

    Answer: D. Notices familiar parts first, then decodes the unfamiliar parts

    According to Ehri's continuum, option A is the logographic phase, option B is the novice alphabetic phase, option C is the mature alphabetic phase, and option D is the orthographic phase. D is the correct choice.

(Average) (Skill 5.5)

67. The most appropriate ESOL strategy for readers who do not read in their L1 is to:

   A. Postpone reading until the ELLs acquire intermediate oral language proficiency

   B. Teach cognates and high-frequency words

   C. Develop literacy in L1 first

   D. Use pull-out reading support in L2

   Answer: C. Develop literacy in L1 first

   Once the ELL understands pre-reading strategies and how the written word is connected to the spoken word, the learner is ready to read. Once fluency is achieved in the first language, second language reading instruction can begin and be more successful.

(Rigorous) (Skill 5.5)

68. Which of the following options is considered to be a disadvantage of continuing language L1 development in pre-literate children?

   A. Children will not learn English as quickly if they continue to use their native language

   B. Many literary skills from L1 transfer to L2

   C. More mature cognitive development is achieved

   D. Teachers are able to build on previous knowledge

Answer: A. Children will not learn English as quickly if they continue to use their native language

Options B, C, and D are all advantages of continuing L1 development. Only option A is a disadvantage. The correct answer is A.

Planning, Implementing, and Managing Instruction

(Average) (Skill 6.1)

69. **Advanced TPR might include:**

   A. Rapid-fire commands

   B. More advanced vocabulary

   C. Funny commands

   D. All of the above

   Answer: D. All of the above

   Total Physical Response can be done slowly, as a beginning activity for ELLs. As they begin to understand more oral English and the game, TPR can be spiced up by all of the suggestions above.

(Rigorous) (Skill 6.1)

70. Which of the following is NOT a step in the Language Experience Approach?

   A. Students draw a picture to represent something personal about an experience

   B. Students dictate their story to the teacher

   C. The teacher reads the story, revising where necessary

   D. The story is read in later days as a follow-up activity

Answer: C. The teacher reads the story, revising where necessary

In the Language Experience Approach, the teacher writes the revised sentences on the storyboard, making the necessary corrections at this time.

(Easy) (Skill 6.2)

71. **In schools with large immigrant populations of diverse origins, the most commonly used model is:**

    A. Submersion

    B. Pull-out

    C. SDAIE

    D. Transition

Answer: B. Pull-out

SDAIE, or Specially Designed Academic Programs in English, is the structured immersion model most commonly used in California. The submersion model does not provide the necessary support that ELLs need and is in disfavor. Transition models provide approximately three years of BICS, but frequently leave the LEP with almost no support while learning CALP. Today, the most commonly used model is B, the pull-out model.

(Rigorous) (Skill 6.2)

72. **Widdowson's definition of *use* and *usage* is well demonstrated in which of the following models?**

    A. Canadian French Immersion and Miami-Dade Count models

    B. Submersion with primary language support

    C. Content-based ESL and indigenous language immersion

    D. Communication-based ESL and Grammar-based ESL

Answer: D. Communication-based ESL and Grammar-based ESL

Widdowson differentiated between how the grammar of a language is reflected in its *usage* and a language's actual *use* in communication.

(Average) (Skill 7.2)

73. **In teaching adults, which of the following is a valid reason for using games?**

    A. To relieve tension

    B. To lighten up a heavy lesson

    C. To allow students to learn in a different mode

    D. All of the above

Answer: D. All of the above

All of the options are valid reasons for incorporating games and game-like activities into the ESOL lesson; therefore, option D is the correct answer.

(Average) (Skill 7.3)

74. **Which of the following reasons is an advantage of using machines in the ESOL classroom?**

    A. They are inexpensive

    B. They are nonjudgmental

    C. They are fun

    D. They are better than teachers

    Answer: B. They are nonjudgmental

    Options A and D are highly doubtful. Option C is questionable. Many educational technology programs are fun; using the equipment itself can be challenging. Only option B is a valid reason for using educational technologies in the language classroom. B is the correct choice.

(Rigorous) (Skill 7.4)

75. **Which one of the following teaching practices has a positive effect on student writing?**

    A. Correction of spelling mistakes

    B. Use of good reading texts

    C. Extensive writing practice

    D. Correction of grammar mistakes

    Answer: B. Use of good reading texts

    Options A, C, and D have had disappointing results in improving student writing. Option B, the use of good reading texts, is the one method to improve writing validated by research. B is the correct choice.

(Average) (Skill 7.5)

76. **Why would the average German- or French-speaking ELL need extra work on the English vowels?**

    A. English vowels are different from L1 of German and French speakers

    B. There is no sound-symbol correspondence in the English vowels

    C. The sound-symbol connection is consistent in both German and French

    D. English has multiple vowel sounds

    Answer: D. English has multiple vowel sounds

    In both German and French, the sound (phoneme)-symbol (grapheme) is consistent, so option C may be discarded. Option A may be eliminated because the vowels are the same in all three languages. There is some sound-symbol correspondence in English, but not always, so option B is incorrect. Option D is the best choice because there are multiple vowel sounds represented by the English vowels and consonants.

(Rigorous) (Skill 7.6)

77. **Which one of the following is a strategy used in content-based learning?**

    A. Teaching phonics for spelling tests

    B. Teaching grammar points discretely

    C. Providing comprehensible feedback

    D. Using activities for fun only

Answer: C. Providing comprehensible feedback

The key to content-based learning is incorporating content-related learning into activities while instructing the needed language skills. Options A, B, and D do not reflect the unity between content and language skills teaching, and, therefore, may be eliminated. The best choice is C, which implies a relationship between the content and its instructional strategy.

(Average) (Skill 7.7)

78. **Angela needs help in English. Her teacher suggested several things Angela can do to improve her learning strategies. Which of the following is NOT a socioaffective learning strategy?**

    A. Read a funny book

    B. Work cooperatively with her classmates

    C. Ask the teacher to speak more slowly

    D. Skim for information

Answer: D. Skim for information

Options A, B and C are all socioaffective learning strategies. Answer D is a cognitive strategy and the correct choice.

(Rigorous) (Skill 7.8)

79. **The Schema Theory of Carrell & Eisterhold suggests that for learning to take place, teachers must:**

    A. Integrate content areas with ESOL techniques

    B. Emphasize all four language skills

    C. Present comprehensible input in a meaningful context

    D. Relate new materials to previous knowledge

Answer: D. Relate new materials to previous knowledge

The Schema Theory of Carrell & Eisterhold suggests that schemata must be related to previous knowledge or learning does not take place. When activated, schemata are able to evaluate the new materials in light of previous knowledge. If the arguments made are convincing to the learner, he or she accepts them and integrates the new knowledge into his or her databank. Otherwise, the new materials are unconvincing, and the new knowledge is rejected by the learner.

(Average) (Skill 7.8)

80. **Incorporating prior knowledge into L2 learning does NOT:**

    A. Permit readers to learn and remember more

    B. Create poor readers

    C. Help readers to evaluate new arguments

    D. Improve comprehension

Answer: B. Create poor readers

Activating schemata and incorporating previous knowledge into L2 learning will strengthen the learning process. It certainly does not create poor readers.

(Average) (Skill 7.9)

81. Instruction to promote fluency includes:

   A. Developing writing and reading skills separately

   B. Explicit study of vocabulary lists

   C. Role play, phonics instruction, and journal writing

   D. Learning only the specific language for the task at hand

   Answer: C. Role play, phonics instruction, and journal writing

   Answers A, B, and D may be discarded as options because they are all poor ESOL techniques. Only answer C suggests various ways in which fluency is developed by constant practice in nonthreatening ways.

(Average) (Skill 8.2)

82. When planning instruction, Ms. Jones provides her students with various materials on the same subject. Which of the following statements is a valid reason for doing so?

   A. It's easier than summarizing all the material

   B. Children like looking at pictures, and some of the textbooks have few pictures

   C. I believe they should have to work to fill in their Know-Want-Learn charts

   D. No two people learn alike, so I try to provide different materials so everyone has something they like

Answer: D. No two people learn alike, so I try to provide different materials so everyone has something they like

Conscientious teachers would reject options A and B as unprofessional. Option C is a valid teaching strategy, but could cause unnecessary difficulty for the task. The best option is D.

(Average) (Skill 8.3)

83. Realia often are used in classrooms. Which one of the following would be a valid example of realia for teaching fractions?

   A. A computer

   B. A balance scale

   C. A white mouse

   D. A pizza

Answer: D. A pizza

A, B, and C are examples of realia that could be used for different purposes. However, dividing a pizza is a sure-fire way to capture the interest of students and initiate the concept of fractions. Answer D is the best choice.

(Rigorous) (Skill 9.1)

84. Young children are often considered better language learners than older children or adults, but older children or adults may be able to progress more rapidly in reading instruction because:

   A. They have more worldly experience to help them understand the texts

   B. Their vocabulary concepts in L2 are less developed

   C. They have more language-learning experience

   D. Phonics is the same in L1 and L2

   Answer: A. They have more worldly experience to help them understand texts

   Answers B and C would depend on the individuals involved in the learning situation. Answer D can readily be discarded because sounds are what distinguish many languages from one another. The correct answer is A. Older learners can apply their worldly experience and schemata developed in L1 to understanding L2 texts as well as other language-learning situations.

(Rigorous) (Skill 9.1)

85. Abigail is an enthusiastic child who spontaneously cries when watching movies. She challenges the teacher in class but is content to let her classmates make decisions. Which of these learning styles most accurately describes her?

   A. Analytic

   B. Authority-oriented

   C. Communicative

   D. Concrete

Answer: D. Concrete

Analytic (A) students are object-oriented, so this option may be discarded. An authority-oriented (B) student would not challenge the teacher, so option B may be discarded. A communicative (C) student likes making decisions and social learning situations. Abigail does not like making decisions, so option C can be eliminated. The best choice is D, concrete learning style, where the learner is people-oriented, emotional, and spontaneous.

(Rigorous) (Skill 9.1)

86. Which of the following should be done prior to initiating a formal referral process for an ELL with possible learning disabilities?

   A. A vision and hearing test

   B. A language diagnostic test

   C. Documentation of at least one intervention

   D. Consultation with the principal about the ELL's progress

   Answer: A. A vision and hearing test

   Answer A is the correct selection because it eliminates the possibility of a childhood health issue before classifying the problem as a learning disorder.

(Rigorous) (Skill 9.1)

87. A fifth grader has completed one year in the ESOL program but does not seem to be making progress. Which of the following might indicate a learning disability?

    A. Frequent code switches

    B. Needing extra time to answer questions

    C. Ability to decode successfully but difficulty in comprehension

    D. Dropping of the final consonants of words

    Answer: C. Ability to decode successfully but difficulty in comprehension

    Answers A and B are normal ELL reactions to the stress of learning a new language. Answer D refers to a pronunciation error that may be normal in the ELL's first language. Only C goes beyond the normal problems of ESOL and possibly into the realm of learning difficulties.

(Rigorous) (Skill 11.2)

88. An ELL suspected of having learning difficulties:

    A. May present behavioral problems when asked to produce written work

    B. May demonstrate the ability to learn quickly

    C. Should be analyzed for up to ten weeks using ESOL techniques

    D. May demonstrate the ability to solve problems not dependent on English

Answer: C. Should be analyzed for up to ten weeks using ESOL techniques

Answers B and D indicate ability beyond the realm of language-learning difficulties; they suggest gifted exceptionalities. Answer A suggests the ELL may be acting out to avoid producing work that is challenging or too difficult. The correct answer would be C, which indicates carefully documented follow-up to avoid placing an ELL in the incorrect environment.

(Rigorous) (Skill 9.1)

89. An ELL student may pronounce /free/ instead of /three/. This is an example of:

    A. Omission

    B. Substitution

    C. Distortion

    D. Addition

    Answer: C. Distortion

    In distortion, the ELL pronounces the phoneme incorrectly and *distorts* the sound.

(Average) (Skill 9.2)

90. Which one of the following policies on classroom management should NOT be established in the classroom by a good classroom manager?

    A. A set of rules

    B. Private talks with different students

    C. Cooperative work groups

    D. Ability groups for regular daily tasks

Answer: D. Ability groups for regular daily tasks

Options A, B, and C are all good classroom management strategies. Only option D has negative effects on students.

(Easy) (Skill 9.3)

91. When the teacher is correcting a student's language, the teacher should:

    A. Carefully correct all mistakes

    B. Consider the context of the error

    C. Confirm the error by repeating it

    D. Repeat the student's message but correct it

Answer: D. Repeat the student's message but correct it

To carefully correct all mistakes a student makes (A) would raise the affective filter and probably cause the student to hesitate before speaking. Considering the context of the error (B) gives the teacher insight into the student's learning, but isn't a method of correction. To confirm the error by repeating it (C) would suggest to the student that his or her utterance was correct and would not be good practice. The best option is D, which corrects the error but in a way that shows the student the correct form without embarrassing him or her.

(Rigorous) (Skill 9.3)

92. Research shows that error correction for ELLs is a delicate business. Which of the following contributes to learning?

    A. Correcting semantic errors

    B. Correcting grammatical errors

    C. Correcting pronunciation

    D. Correcting all written work errors

Answer: A. Correcting semantic errors

The correction of semantic errors leads to increased vocabulary and L2 learning. All other options have been proven to be ineffective.

(Rigorous) (Skill 9.4)

93. The content teacher is trying to establish a text-rich classroom, including some bilingual material. Why is this important to all students?

    A. It emphasizes the importance of reading

    B. It is motivational

    C. It is welcoming

    D. All of the above

Answer: D. All of the above

Option A stresses the importance of reading. Option B suggests that a text-rich environment is motivational for readers. Option C is a nonthreatening way to welcome students of other cultures and make them feel comfortable in their new classroom. Option D is the correct answer.

(Rigorous) (Skill 9.5)

94. Which of the following activities is the most effective in learning to use the dictionary effectively?

    A. Locating synonyms, phrases, and etymology of words

    B. Looking up definitions and writing a sentence with the words

    C. Rewriting the definition in your own words

    D. Writing down the pronunciation guide and the definition

    Answer: A. Locating synonyms, phrases, and etymology of words

    According to Schumm, options B, C, and D do not allow the learner to fully explore the parts of a dictionary and how to use it. Option A provides the student with additional information about the word and the range of information available in a dictionary. Option A is the best choice.

Assessment

(Rigorous) (Skill 10.1)

95. Which of the following tests is NOT a state-mandated test or a reading/language arts basic skill test?

    A. DRA

    B. WIDA

    C. Iowa Test of Basic Skills

    D. TOEIC

Answer: D. TOEIC

Option A is the Pearson Developmental Reading Assessment (DRA). Option B is the World-Class Instructional Design and Assessment (WIDA) test. Option C tests basic language arts skills. Option D is the Test of English for International Communication by the Educational Testing Service (ETS).

(Rigorous) (Skill 10.2)

96. What is the main purpose of Title I?

    A. To test the English level of ELLs

    B. To establish guidelines for the classification of ELLs entering new schools

    C. To establish guidelines for the AYP report

    D. To provide funds to states to support programs for students who need help in math and reading

Answer: D. To provide funds to states to support programs for students who need help in math and reading

Option A is not the purpose of Title I; placement tests are used for this purpose. Options B and C are elements of the NCLB Act. Option D is a goal of Title I; it is the best choice.

(Rigorous) (Skill 10.4)

97. Which one of the following is NOT an authentic way to confirm standardized placement testing results?

    A. Diagnostic tests

    B. Teacher observations

    C. Previous school records

    D. Oral interviews

Answer: A. Diagnostic tests

Answer A is correct because diagnostic tests are used to determine a student's abilities. They are typically administered by psychologists or speech therapists in clinical settings when specific language learning problems are present.

(Average) (Skill 10.6)

98. Which of the following is NOT an acceptable alternative assessment strategy for ELLs?

   A. Portfolios

   B. Observation

   C. Self-assessment

   D. Essay writing

Answer: D. Essay writing

Answer D is the correct response because essay writing is not an appropriate strategy for evaluating the English capabilities of ELLs.

(Average) (Skill 11.1)

99. Which of the following accommodations may be allowed for ELLs during assessment?

   A. Having a translator explain difficult words

   B. Asking proctor to explain certain words or test items

   C. Paraphrasing the prompt

   D. Allowing the use of an English-heritage language translating dictionary

Answer: D. Allowing the use of an English-heritage language translating dictionary

Answers A, B, and C would defeat the purpose of assessing the ELLs. Answer D is an appropriate accommodation during assessment.

(Rigorous) (Skill 11.2)

100. Which of the following is NOT an acceptable teaching practice when preparing exceptional students to take tests?

   A. Give practice timed tests

   B. Use cloze tests

   C. Provide students with study guides

   D. Have the students write practice essays

Answer: D. Have the students write practice essays

Answer D is the correct response because essay writing is not an appropriate strategy for evaluating exceptionality.

(Average) (Skill 11.2)

101. Which of the following is a possible sign of a gifted ELL student?

   A. Normal development according to parental interview

   B. Speech delayed in L2

   C. Seems to solve logic problems with difficulty

   D. High academic performance in L1

Answer: D. High academic performance in L1

Answer D suggests that excellent academic work in their first language would be the prime indicator of students with exceptional abilities, especially if it is also apparent in the L2.

(Rigorous) (Skill 11.3)

102. **Which is the most appropriate method for dealing with a potential cultural bias in tests?**

    A. Translate the tests previous to the actual exam

    B. Provide pictures and graphics during the test

    C. Administer practice tests with time limits

    D. Provide a study guide and give the test orally

Answer: C. Administer practice tests with time limits

Answers A, B, and D are accommodations for the language deficiencies of ELLs, but do not address cultural bias. Answer C addresses cultural bias because many cultures do not time tests. ELLs may find this a difficulty because it is a norm in many U.S. testing environments.

(Rigorous) (Skill 11.3)

103. **If a test question asks a student about a Wii video game, which kind of bias may it contain?**

    A. Cultural

    B. Attitudinal

    C. Test/norming

    D. Translation

Answer: A. Cultural

Option B refers to the attitude of the examiner towards a certain language, dialect, or culture. Option C occurs when ELLs are excluded in the school's population when obtaining norm results. Option D concerns translation bias caused by translating literally and possibly losing the essence of the test item. Only option A refers to the assumption that all students and cultures are familiar with the normal experiences of a middle-class North American child. A is the best choice.

(Rigorous) (Skill 11.4)

104. **When ELLs are asked to fill in the blanks/gaps on a multiple-choice test, which type of test are they being given?**

    A. First generation

    B. Second generation

    C. Third generation

    D. Traditional

Answer: A. First generation

Second generation (B) and traditional (D) tests are the same. They are long, discrete point tests with no connection between the test items. Option C, third generation tests, are tests that set an integrated task for the test taker, such as listening for information about an arriving train. Option A, first generation tests, are those based on the grammar-translation method of teaching. Students are set tasks such as writing an essay or answering multiple-choice questions. Answer A is the correct answer.

(Rigorous) (Skill 12.1)

105. **Which of the following is a feature of differentiated instruction?**

    A. The teacher plans what all students will learn

    B. The students are placed in learning levels

    C. The gifted student is given a list of learning objectives

    D. Materials are grouped according to ability levels

Answer: A. The teacher plans what all students will learn

Option D may be discounted because all materials are available to all students. Option C can be eliminated because all students are allowed to pursue the learning activity as deeply as they wish. Option B may be eliminated because established ability grouping is a demotivating factor for students. The correct selection is A: The teacher establishes learning goals for all students and allows them to pursue the content according to their interests and abilities.

Cultural and Professional Aspects of the Job

(Average) (Skill 13.1)

106. **Culture and cultural differences:**

    A. Must be addressed by the teacher in the ELL classroom by pointing out cultural similarities and differences

    B. Should be the starting point for learning about how culture affects the ELL's attitude towards education

    C. Positively affects how well ELLs perform in the language classroom

    D. May have a strong emotional influence on the ELL learner

Answer: D. Mmay have a strong emotional influence on the ELL learner

Culture and cultural differences may be addressed by the skillful ESOL teacher, but frequently teachers are unaware of all the cultures and cultural differences with which they are dealing. At the same time, it may be possible to determine how his or her culture affects the ELL's attitude towards education, but it may well be something the young child cannot express or the adult hides for various reasons. Culture and cultural differences do not always play a positive role in the learning process. Culture and cultural differences may have a strong emotional influence— either positive or negative—on the ELL learner. Thus, D is the best option.

(Rigorous) (Skill 13.3)

107. **ESOL instruction frequently requires the teacher to change her instruction methods. One of the most difficult may be the:**

    A. Wait time

    B. Establishment of group work

    C. Show-and-tell based on different cultures

    D. Extensive reading time

Answer: A. Wait time

Answer B, C, and D can all be discounted because they are standard practice for language arts teachers. Answer A, the amount of time a teacher waits for an answer from her students, can be very difficult to change. Teachers may be somewhat impatient ("Let's get on with it"), lack understanding ("If they knew the answer, they would respond"), and unaware of differences between the U.S. and other cultures. Answer A is the correct response.

(Rigorous) (Skill 13.3)

108. **When Mr. Smith planned his class on plants, he brought in plants and a series of lectures using PowerPoint. His class most likely contains many learners of which of the following types?**

    A. Tactile

    B. Auditory

    C. Kinesthetic

    D. Visual

Answer: D. Visual

Option A, tactile learners, would enjoy touching the plants. Option B, auditory learners, would appreciate listening to lectures accompanying the PowerPoint presentation. Option C, kinesthetic learners, need movement to learn well so this option may be discarded. Showing a plant and a PowerPoint presentation will appeal to visual learners, option D. This is the best choice.

(Rigorous) (Skill 13.7)

109. Which of the following suggestions would the culturally aware teacher disregard, if necessary?

    A. The use of English only in the classroom

    B. Creating a "safe haven" for refugees and at-risk students

    C. Free discussions with women from Muslim cultures

    D. Shaking hands with all parents

Answer: A. The use of English only in the classroom

The culturally aware teacher would embrace Option B. Options C and D are culturally bound, and it would be inappropriate to engage in these behaviors unless invited to do so. Teachers who know their students' language may judiciously use it in the classroom to demonstrate respect for and knowledge of other cultures. Option A is the best choice.

(Average) (Skill 13.8)

110. Social factors influence second-language learning because:

    A. Age determines how much one learns

    B. Gender roles are predetermined

    C. Social status is important to the ELL's ability to perform well in the learning situation

    D. Many ELLs cannot ignore their social conditions

Answer: D. Many ELLs cannot ignore their social conditions

Motivation, whether a trait (state) or a state (instrumental), is probably the most powerful element in the acquisition of a second language. Without family or community support, the ELL may be under tremendous pressure and feel threatened by the new language. For him or her to succeed, he or she must do so at considerable personal sacrifice.

(Rigorous) (Skill 14.1)

111. In *Lau v. Nichols* (1974), the Supreme Court ruled that:

    A. School districts may not continue education programs that fail to produce positive results for ELLs

    B. Sexual harassment is prohibited in any school activity on or off campus

    C. Students were denied an "equal" education

    D. Discrimination against students and employers based on race, ethnicity, national origins, disability, or marital status is prohibited

Answer: C. Students were denied an "equal" education

Answer A refers to *Castaneda v. Pickard* (1981). Answer B refers to Title IX of the Education Amendments of 1972. Answer D was covered in the Florida Educational Equity Act of 1984. Only option C refers to *Lau v. Nichols* (1974).

(Rigorous) (Skill 14.2)

112. Which of the following is NOT appropriate when setting high standards for ELLs?

    A. The use of cooperative learning strategies between teacher and students

    B. Establishing goals to accommodate all ELLs

    C. Challenging students cognitively

    D. Developing language and literacy through all instructional activities

Answer: B. Establishing goals to accommodate all ELLs

Options A, C, and D are appropriate principles for establishing high standards for all ELLs. Option B is the correct answer because it implies lowering the standards to accommodate some ELLs.

(Rigorous) (Skill 14.3)

113. The No Child Left Behind Act established that:

    A. Title I funds are available only if the schools participate in National Assessment of Education Progress

    B. Bilingual programs must be effective and follow three criteria established by a federal court in 1981

    C. High-performing children cannot be used to average out low-performing ELLs

    D. Schools must form and convene assessment committees

Answer: C. High-performing children cannot be used to average out low-performing ELLs

Option A refers to the establishment of voluntary school participation in NAEP after the National Committee on Excellence in Education produced their report, *A Nation at Risk* (1983). Option B refers to the decision rendered in *Castaneda v. Pickard* (1981). One requirement resulting from *Lau v. Nichols* (1974) was that schools must form and convene assessment committees (D). The NCLB act specifically states that disaggregated data must be used in evaluating school performance (C).

(Rigorous) (Skill 14.3)

114. The No Child Left Behind Act requires schools to:

    A. Give assessment in English if the LEP has received 3 years of schooling in the U.S. (except for Puerto Rico)

    B. Measure school districts by status

    C. Inform parents of the school's evaluation

    D. Include LEPs in all academic assessments

Answer: A. Give assessment in English if the LEP has received 3 years of schooling in the U.S. (except for Puerto Rico)

Because NCLB requires schools to focus on quality education for students who were often overlooked by the educational system in general, LEPs with three years of schooling must be tested in English.

(Average) (Skills 7.1, 15.1)

115. **What is the teacher's most important role in student-centered learning?**

    A. Mentor

    B. Facilitator

    C. Guide

    D. Model

Answer: B Facilitator

All of the options are roles of the teacher in communication-based learning. Because the teacher must step back and place the students' needs first in student-based learning, she needs to facilitate the students' needs through careful planning to achieve the unit objectives and to help the students create rubrics for evaluation. Option B, facilitator, is the best choice.

(Rigorous) (Skill 15.3)

116. **The affective filter affects how students acquire a second language because:**

    A. Learning a second language may make the learner feel vulnerable

    B. The attitude of peers and family is motivating

    C. Motivation is a powerful personal factor

    D. Facilitative anxiety determines our reaction to competition and is positive

Answer: A. Learning a second language may make the learner feel vulnerable

The affective filter is the full range of human feelings and emotions that come into play during second-language acquisition. Learning a second language may make the learner vulnerable because he or she may have to leave his or her comfort zone behind. This can be especially difficult for adults who are used to being "powerful" or "in control" in their professions, but also affects children and teens. Option A is the best selection.

(Rigorous) (Skill 15.3)

117. **Which of the following personality traits is a "facilitative" anxiety?**

    A. Inability to speak before peers

    B. Discrimination

    C. Completes tasks on time

    D. Fear of classmates ridicule

Answer: C. Completes tasks on time

Option A, shyness, may cause students to be afraid of speaking before their classmates who might ridicule them (D). Both are examples of *debilitating* anxiety. If ELLs are discriminated against (B) in school because of their accent or culture, then they too may suffer from *debilitating* anxiety. Only option C, completes tasks on time (whether because of fear of punishment or a desire to acquire new knowledge), suggests facilitative anxiety, which encourages the student to accomplish goals. Option C is the best choice.

(Rigorous) (Skill 15.5)

118. Transitioning from one class to another or one school to another is challenging for most students. Which of the following activities would NOT make the process easier for most students?

    A. Visiting the new classroom/school

    B. Holding a parental orientation session

    C. Holding a Q&A session with students from the new school

    D. Conducting a Q&A session with the present teachers

Answer: D. Conducting a Q&A session with the present teachers

Options A, B, and C are all recommended practices to ease the transition worries. Option D is less effective because the present teachers are known factors and do not represent the new and unknown venue or people of the new class/school. Option D is the best choice.

(Average) (Skill 15.9)

119. When communicating with parents or caregivers about a student's progress, the teacher should:

    A. Establish grading policies for each assignment

    B. Send notes home well in advance of field trips

    C. Develop rubrics, send them home, and have parents sign and return them

    D. Send notes home about school events when the new term begins

Answer: C. Develop rubrics, send them home, and have parents sign and return them

Option A is a good policy for teachers, but does not mention of sharing this policy with the parents or caregivers. Option B only concerns field trips and is not about progress of the student. Option D is informative about school events and not about student progress. Option C may seem like overkill, but it does establish firm grading policies that are shared, in advance, with the parents or caregivers. C is the best option.

(Rigorous) (Skill 16.2)

120. Which of the following sources would be the most appropriate when inquiring about cultural issues concerning ELLs?

    A. *http://www2.ed.gov/about/offices/list/ies/index.html?src=oc*

    B. *http://www.ed.gov/offices/OCR*

    C. *http://www.cal.org*

    D. *http://www.nabe.org*

Answer: A. *http://www2.ed.gov/about/offices/list/ies/index.html?src=oc*

Option D is the web address of National Association of Bilingual Education. Option C is the web address of the Center for Applied Linguistics (CAL). Option B is the web address of the Office for Civil Rights (OCR). Option A is the web address of the United States Department of Education, Office of English Language Acquisition (OELA). Option A would be the best choice, though depending on the exact nature of the investigation, other venues could be of help.